OMENS
FROM YOUR
DREAMS

AN A-Z TO THE MYSTERIES OF SLEEP

PHILIPPA WARING

Illustrated with engravings by
Thomas Bewick

CHANCELLOR
PRESS

This 1993 edition published in Great Britain
by Chancellor Press
an imprint of Reed Consumer Books Limited
Michelin House, 81 Fulham Road, London SW3 6RB
and Auckland, Melbourne, Singapore and Toronto

Copyright © 1991 Souvenir Press Ltd.
ISBN 1 85152 270 0

A CIP catalogue record for this book is available
at the British Library

Printed in the Slovak Republic
50964

INTRODUCTION

Scientific research has shown that we human beings spend one-third of our lives asleep, and during the average lifetime we dream for at least 50,000 hours. Small wonder, then, that dreams and their meanings should be regarded as one of the most intriguing aspects of life . . . as well as one of the most mysterious.

Since humanity first began to wonder about the nature of things, people have puzzled over the meaning of these 'visions of the night'. It is probable that dream lore evolved in prehistoric times, but certainly with evidence to hand that is at least 4,000 years old, there can be no doubting the enduring fascination of the subject.

Plato, the famous Athenian philosopher and one of the pioneers of dream research, wrote almost 2,000 years ago: 'There exists in every one of us, even in some of those reputed most respectable, a terrible, fierce and lawless brood of desires, which it seems are revealed in sleep.' Echoing these words a century ago, the German philosopher Friedrich Nietzsche declared, 'Nothing contains more of your own work than your dreams. Nothing belongs to you so much.' Only last year the Scottish psychiatrist Dr Colin Shapiro reported after researching the dreams of 1,500 people, 'Countless important tasks are being performed in sleep, many of which we just don't understand but which have physiological and psychological significance'.

Although with each passing year research is steadily drawing aside the veils on the mysteries of sleep, it has also shown that dreams are rather like icebergs — they show on the surface of our memories only a little of the reality that preceded them. Hence our overwhelming desire to interpret the omens that they undeniably contain.

The results of recent enquiries into sleep have suggested that children dream more than adults, but the middle-aged and elderly who sleep for shorter, more disturbed periods, dream most of all. Interestingly, too, the things women dream about are mostly very different to men, and their dreams are more often located indoors than outdoors, and in familiar surroundings. In men's dreams, by far the largest number feature physical action of one sort or another.

Further, it has been estimated that we dream for about a quarter of the time we are asleep and may well have as many as six dreams a night — each of which probably lasts for a maximum of about 15 minutes. Researchers have also stated that most of our dreams are actually rather dull and uninteresting, and it is only those which are vivid or bizarre that leave any kind of memory in the consciousness. These memories take the form of feelings or symbols, and it is they which have fascinated and absorbed writers on dreams since the days of the ancient Egyptians and beyond.

The oldest dream book extant is a papyrus preserved in the British Museum which relates to the 12th Egyptian dynasty between the years 2000–1790 BC. It was found in the library of clay tablets of the last great Assyrian king, Ashurbanipal, and reveals the art of dream interpretation to have been already well developed at this early period in human history. Indeed, the writings of Joseph, the son of Jacob, who interpreted the dreams of some of the Pharaohs, are also ascribed to around this same period.

4

The signs are, though, that early man believed his dreams were revelations from the gods — a theory certainly substantiated in the literature of the ancient Babylonians, Egyptians, Greeks, and Romans. Indeed, in Homer's *Iliad*, Achilles says, 'For dreams, too, are sent by Zeus', and in the Bible, at Numbers 12:6, the Lord declares, 'If there be a prophet among you, I the Lord will make myself known unto him in a vision, and will speak unto him in a dream.' (*King James Version*).

With the passage of time such beliefs naturally declined, though the interest in dreams and their omens redoubled. In the second century BC, a Roman soothsayer, Artemidorus of Daldis, began collecting from the writings of others, and from local folklore, all he could find about dreams; and published a monumental work of five volumes entitled *Interpretation of Dreames*. On the evidence of this work, Artemidorus may be regarded as the 'father of dream books'; although it seems likely that other scribes in China, India and the Arab world, were also busy then interpreting the visions of sleep.

Another important work, *Discourse on Dreams*, was written in the fourth century AD by Synesius of Cyrene who, though he borrowed from Artemidorus, took the trouble to urge his readers to write down what they remembered, being careful not to overlook any details, for 'by images we conjecture the action of the future'.

In the thirteenth century, the Spanish appointed the philosopher Arnald of Villanova the first 'official dream interpreter' to the court of Aragon and he compiled the legendary *Expositiones Visionum*. Then at the beginning of the Renaissance, an Italian, Geronimo Cardano, wrote a fascinating treatise about the famous dreams experienced by warriors and kings that had subsequently decided important events.

By the Middle Ages, dreams had became the subject of an ever-increasing number of dream books and tables, many of which it has to be said interpreted the experiences by the crudest rules of thumb. However, the sixteenth century saw the coming of enlightenment, and the publication of another ground-breaking work, *The Dream Book of Daniel*, first published in Venice and later translated into all the major European languages. It was a determined attempt to distinguish between divine, natural, and diabolical dreams, and by so doing set a pattern which has continued to this day.

Succeeding centuries brought about the publication of several more famous studies (or infamous, depending on your viewpoint), such as Gabdorrachaman's *Arabic Dream Lore* (1664), *The New Book of Knowledge* (1767), *The Royal Dream Book* (1780), *Raphael's Dream Book* (1830), and *Napoleon's Book of Fate* (1880). Nor was this interest just confined to Europe, for a series of similar volumes followed the lead of the first American dream book, *The Universal Interpreter of Dreams and Visions*, after its publication in Baltimore in 1795.

It was in 1900, of course, that Sigmund Freud brought out his classic work, *The Interpretation of Dreams*, and instigated the school of dream research which has continued with increasing vigour and success to the present time. In this book, Freud advanced the theory that dreams represented repressed drives and emotional conflicts in the dreamer's subconscious, that surfaced during sleep as recognisable symbols. Though his theory is still accepted today by many psychologists and psychiatrists, few accept it in its entirety because it has become apparent that a great deal of dreaming is too prosaic to have any deep emotional significance.

It is obviously not possible, in a work such as this, to discuss all that has been achieved in dream research in the years since Freud's pioneer work — indeed a considerable number of articles and books have already done just that — but it does need to be stated that the entries in this dictionary have been based on the results of the most recent enquiry in Britain, America and Europe. These are considered alongside some of the most anciently recorded traditions, and thus demonstrates the longevity and interest in the topic.

Almost all of the other dream books that I have studied have taken a very unequivocal line in stating their interpretation of each different dream. I, on the other hand, have chosen to combine the accumulated wisdom of the centuries, with the pronouncements of the most recent enquiry to enable the reader to have a wide range of interpretations at his disposal. And rather than attempt to cover countless thousands of subjects, I have concentrated on a total of just under 600 of the most frequently and widely reported dreams.

Research has now clearly established that dream 'storylines' are usually so distorted as to make very little sense. Because of this, most dreamers on awaking, endeavour to make some sense of what they have experienced, perhaps even attempting to 'finish' the dream. But what, in fact, is far more important in determining the meaning of a dream is to establish its location and atmosphere — were the feelings those of happiness or hostility? — and to recall any particular symbol or motif that made a vivid impression on the mind. Because the natural language of the brain is said to be symbolic, the likelihood is that the dream has a meaning beyond the obvious interpretation; although I should stress that a literal interpretation should never be overlooked as a first possibility. Once the dreamer has collated this basic information, he or she should refer to the appropriate entry in this book.

During the time I was engaged in my research, I was interested to discover that unhappiness, defeat, and failure occur more often in dreams than contentment and success; while hostile and aggressive encounters are more frequent than friendly contact. Of all the different types of dreams, four are apparently more commonplace than any other, in Western society at least: they are dreams of sex, nakedness, falling and flying. Why this should be so is another of the mysteries of sleep.

A few years ago, the English poet and philosopher W. H. Auden, doubtless having just experienced a particularly vivid dream, wrote, 'Learn from your dreams what you lack'. In the pages which follow I have drawn on 4,000 years of study and interpretation to try to provide just such a solution for any curious dreamer.

I wish you pleasant dreams!

Philippa Waring
Suffolk, England
1991

A

ABANDONED
The sensation of being abandoned in a dream was first noted by the Chinese who claimed it was symbolic of indecision about the future. The Arabs, however, felt it prophesied a long life, and subsequent sources have continued to vary the omens. In sixteenth-century Europe, to dream of abandoning a relative or friend presaged an illness, while 200 years later it was a warning against foolish actions. More recent research has claimed it is actually a dream of contrary: a reunion with someone who was once close is about to take place. A British authority has also suggested the dreamer may be subconsciously afraid of losing a loved one and should do more to cement the relationship.

ABBEY
To dream of an abbey, or any great Christian religious building such as a cathedral or monastery, has been considered throughout Europe as an omen of peace of mind and security since the Middle Ages. Sixteenth-century sources claimed that to dream of being refused admission to such a place would result in the dreamer being prevented from making a terrible mistake, though to imagine conversing with anyone in an abbey, particularly a member of the Church, indicated 'committing a terrible sin'. A ruined abbey signifies the spoiling of plans, while a recent study

has suggested the dream is symbolic of a nostalgic yearning for the tranquillity of the past.

ABORIGINE
The Australian Aborigines have a tradition of dream lore that is one of the most ancient in the world and recent study has shown that a number of their beliefs match those of other races and nations. Dreams of Aborigines themselves — in company with any other native peoples, for that matter — have been a feature of dream almanacs for the past two centuries. Some nineteenth-century European authorities, for instance, warned female readers that dreams of 'native savages' were symbolic of sexual temptation, while an even stronger prejudice was evidenced in certain turn-of-the-century American almanacs which declared that dreams of black women were symbolic of 'unnatural passions'! Today, authorities are agreed that all such dreams are symptomatic of a desire for a simpler, happier and less sophisticated life.

ABORTION
Dreams about abortion have been widely reported in the last fifty years, but records of earlier instances are few and far between. A lone Victorian source, for instance, indicated that such a dream presaged 'troubles ahead', while a French almanac published in the early 1900s claimed it intimated the end of a love-affair. Recent American research has suggested the dream has equal application for men and woman, predicting loneliness and failure; while a British authority believes it is symbolic of a refusal to face up to a deep-seated sexual problem.

ABYSS
Tumbling into an abyss or pit is one of the most frightening of dream experiences, and both early Greek and Roman sources mentioned the sensation and agreed it was symbolic of problems ahead. In the East, the dream was

specifically related to business and money worries, and the longer the fall the greater the decline in fortune — although in the case of women it could signify sorrow and ill-health. More recently, American almanacs have stated that the dream is a warning to men against lending money as it is unlikely to be returned; and to women a sign of indifference in love. In Britain other sources have suggested that the cause may well be a lack of self-confidence in facing up to difficult decisions.

ACCIDENT
Dreams in which accidents of one kind or another occur have been known since the earliest times and are accepted everywhere as an omen of possible disaster. The most widely recorded accident-dreams relate to travel and the best advice is to avoid the means of transport involved (car, train, aircraft or ship) for at least the next twenty-four hours. Some writers on dreams have suggested that an accident which takes place on a ship should be taken as an omen of a love-affair going on the rocks, while any disaster involving vehicles could indicate that a person's business affairs are about to run off the road. A curious old American dictionary of rural lore claims that any dream in which an accident occurs to cattle 'denotes that you will struggle with all your might to gain some object and then see some friend lose property of the same value in aiding your cause'.

ACCUSED
Dreams of being the subject of accusation are to be found dating back 4,000 years to the time of the ancient Egyptians. Then, such experiences were believed to be a warning to the sleeper about plots being hatched against him. By the Middle Ages, however, they were said to signify a scandal in the making, and only if the dreamer could prove his innocence before awaking would the problem be avoided. Later authorities have claimed that, in general terms, for a man to imagine being accused by a woman points to

business troubles, while in the reverse situation the woman is in for some good news! A recurring dream of being falsely accused means the dreamer's problems undoubtedly require professional help to resolve.

ACROBAT
The acrobat or tumbler has been a part of dream lore since the Middle Ages when to imagine one performing was described as an omen warning the dreamer against making a journey in the next few weeks. Some time later in Europe, the same dream became an indication of overcoming enemies, while in Russia it was said to signify 'the frustrating of plans by the foolishness of others'. A charming Victorian almanac claimed that the young girl who dreamed of acrobats 'would court the favours of men'. More recent study has suggested this is a dream of contrary and to imagine an acrobat being involved in an accident will lead to the dreamer having a lucky escape, although if the sleeper is personally involved it is symbolic of a need to succeed in some particularly demanding scheme.

ACTING
There are strong traditions in America and India about dreams featuring members of the acting profession, and the omens concerning them vary considerably. The most common concerns falling in love with an actor or actress, which is a sign that your talents and inclinations are directed towards pleasure rather than hard work. If a woman dreams of marrying an actor then she may well find regret following any glamorous or superficial pleasure she is currently enjoying in her life; while for a man the dream foretells an unhappy period with his sweetheart or wife. For either sex to dream of being a member of the profession, is a sign that a lot of hard work lies ahead, culminating in satisfaction. Indian lore says that to dream of an actor who is either ill or dead is a sign that the dreamer is going to experience a time of misery; while in America it is thought

that to talk to an actor or actress in your sleep is a warning
not to spread gossip unless you are prepared for dire consequences among your friends. A recent British survey has
suggested the dream is symbolic of self-deception and a
change of life style is probably necessary.

ADDITION
Wrestling with figures is another commonly reported
dream, though not just among those who make their living
in business or as accountants. To dream of struggling with
figures is a sign that a difficult situation — one you may
already know about or suspect — is going to prove hard to
resolve. In China, dream lore says that if the figures in your
additions are indistinct then beware of gambling or speculation because you are sure to lose. In Europe, to solve any
piece of addition in your sleep is believed to indicate you
will foresee a forthcoming problem and be able to handle it;
while a recent American dream survey reported that
anyone who dreamed of adding up figures using a machine
was about to make a good business contact and thereby
avoid some potentially difficult problems. A British authority stated recently that the dream is symbolic of im-
patience, in particular towards personal achievement.

ADOPTION
A dream which relates to adoption in any respect actually
has little to do with the subject. For example, to imagine
that you are adopting a child is an indication you could be
about to make an ill-advised move of your home. Another
old tradition says that to see someone in your dreams, who
you know to be adopted, is a sign that a stranger is about to
play a significant part in your future affairs. More recently,
it has been claimed that if a person who is adopted dreams
about adoption, then he is about to receive an appeal for
help from someone close to him. An American book on
dreams has claimed that to imagine adopting children indicates problems in love, while a British source has also

suggested that the experience is symbolic of lacking someone in life on whom to lavish love and affection.

ADULTERY
One of the oldest topics in dream lore, though most authorities state that to dream of committing adultery with
another man's wife has much broader implications: in general, that the dreamer is in danger of being caught carrying
out some wrongful action in the near future. Curiously,
too, to resist committing adultery in a dream is an omen
that you are about to face some disappointments —
though, happily, they will only be temporary. A nineteenth-century French almanac advises readers who dream
of committing adultery to take this as a warning against
confiding their innermost secrets to a new-found friend for
fear of being hurt. This same book also informs single girls
who dream of adultery that they are about to experience
some strange, but pleasurable adventures. A recent American book of dream lore claimed that to dream of committing
adultery is actually a sign of excellent morals, but if others
are doing it then a loss of money is to be expected!

ADVENTURE
Dreaming is in itself an adventure of the mind, but if the
nature of your experiences while asleep leave the impression of having been rather like a real-life adventure, then it
is your emotional state on waking that will provide the
omens for the future. If you feel elated and happy, then
look ahead for some good times with your family and
friends; but if the emotions are those of depression and
unhappiness then make special efforts with those closest to
you; and watch your business dealings with special care.
Some old books of dream lore used to maintain that anyone
victimised by an adventurer in their dreams was easy prey
for flattery, while the young woman who imagined herself
as a glamorous adventuress should be on her guard against
the wiles of a heartless seducer. Recent research in Britain

14

and America has concluded that the dream symbolises the need for a dramatic change of routine.

ADVERTISEMENTS
A surprisingly commonplace feature in dreaming, according to world-wide reports. To imagine reading advertisements while asleep, is a clear sign that any special plans you may be making are about to take place. If you are aware of illustrations in the advertisements this bodes even better. In America, to dream of placing advertisements in newspapers or magazines is an omen that you are going to have to work particularly hard to achieve your objectives; on the European side of the Atlantic the same dream should be taken as a clear warning against undertaking any speculative scheme. A British authority has also stated that the dream underlines a need to be more forceful in life.

ADVICE
To dream of giving or receiving advice is a dream that has been recorded since antiquity, the omens being remarkably straightforward. To give advice will result in a new friendship, while to imagine receiving it is a warning against being deceived. According to later European sources, a dream of giving advice was also thought to be a sign of a rise in status, though to have to seek legal advice foretold business problems. A German almanac of the seventeenth century stated that getting advice from a priest would result in loneliness, while a more recent American publication says dreaming of giving financial advice will produce a monetary reward!

AGE
A person's age is an enduring subject of interest, and dreams concerning this can be found in the very earliest compilations. One of the most persistent refers to the dreamer who imagines him- or herself older than they actually are — a bad omen, apparently, indicating a

forthcoming failure in some aspect of life. Medical science nowadays, however, believes such a dream to be a warning of encroaching sickness and strongly advises a visit to the doctor. Curiously, to see old people in dreams is a sign of good luck according to the Chinese, for it portends that the dreamer, too, will live to a ripe old age.

AIR
Although air as such rarely appears in dreams, it is, of course, vital in such commonplace experiences as those featuring the weather, the activities of birds, or the sensation of flying. Air is therefore considered as a principle of psychic life, and writers on dream lore have been including entries about it in their work since the sixteenth century. One famous source, *The Dreams of Joseph* (1566), declared that, 'To see air fair and clear promises success to all persons; but to see air dark, misty or cloudy portends the hindrance of actions.' An eighteenth-century European almanac declared that to dream of breathing hot air prophesied coming under evil influences, while cold air would lead to problems in business and domestic affairs. Being oppressed by humidity would lead to a stifling of future plans, it added. Modern research has tended to confirm these definitions, while stressing that the other activities associated with the air in the dream are of paramount importance in determining the omens.

AIRCRAFT
Phallic interpretations have been applied to aircraft by a number of modern writers on dreams: its elongated shape representative of an erection, and the fact that it is hollow with motionless passengers inside also gives it a female component. Being very much an image of the twentieth century, the aircraft is more generally thought to be an omen of swift success — but with its power to leave the earth, although constantly threatened with a fall, it cautions the dreamer about taking undue risks in his everyday

life. To dream of piloting an aircraft is said to foretell a special achievement in life, while to fall or parachute from a plane in flight is a sign of some temporary problems ahead. To imagine being a passenger indicates that some news from far away is imminent; and any flight apparently being made in bad weather should not be seen as a sign of danger to life, but more probably a set-back in business.

ALLEY

To dream of being in an alley is another of those perplexing cases where different countries have different explanations. The Americans, for instance, believe it is symptomatic of a decline in the dreamer's fortunes with many unexpected problems arising; the British, by contrast, feel it signifies an easy road ahead, unless the alley comes to a dead end in which case greater effort to succeed will be required. In several European countries, for a young girl to dream of an alley is a warning to her about making friendships with people of disreputable character. The French, too, believe the dream has special significance for women: a dark alley, they say, symbolises gossip by neighbours.

ALTAR

In many dream books the altar has been regarded as a symbol of marriage since Biblical times; although some sources also speak of it as a warning against committing evil. In the Middle Ages, a dream of an altar being desecrated was regarded as a terrible omen which would lead to the death of a child. Even to sense confusion around an altar was a warning about the activities of enemies. Later European authorities claimed the dream prophesied the realisation of a 'secret desire'. Modern sources tend to believe the dream presages some good news from an unexpected source, and a recent American almanac claimed this would manifest itself in the discovery of some lost money!

AMBUSH

For centuries, dreams in which the sleeper was the victim of an ambush were read as an indication that a hidden danger was lying in wait and could only be avoided by the utmost caution. Many old almanacs make particular mention of this experience, adding that if the sleeper was a part of the ambush it was a warning against participating in any activity which might bring harm to friends. More recently, in America especially, this kind of dream has been taken as an omen that the sleeper is contemplating some action involving others which he or she may have cause to regret.

ANGEL

Angels and winged men are to be found in dreams recorded by the Babylonians as well as in the Bible, and they have continued to be imagined to the present day. Interestingly, female angels are virtually unknown in dreams. According to the earliest sources, the angel is symbolic of wisdom, a messenger of inspiration. By the Middle Ages, they were regarded as a warning against those pursuing evil ways, and a comfort to those seeking a change for the better in their lives. More recent almanacs have described the angel as a symbol of success in love, while several angels signify prosperity. Modern sources believe the dream forecasts happiness and protection in general terms, and to religious people a symbol that they have 'spiritual friends'.

ANIMALS

The earliest sources refer to wild animals in dreams as symbols of danger, though the Assyrians believed them to be a specific warning against the machinations of prominent or influential people. To be attacked or wounded by a wild animal also pointed to serious family problems or an illness. By the Middle Ages, however, this had become a dream of contrary: wild animals were seen as symbolishing long life and prosperity against all the odds. In recent times, the condition of animals has become an important dream omen. A healthy creature points to good fortune in business dealings, while a sickly one indicates a failure in love. The way animals are treated in a dream is also relevant, for creatures which come to be petted represent good friends. Dogs are particularly good omens in dreams for they, too, symbolise friendship and happy times ahead.

ANTIQUES
Dreaming of old furniture and *objets d'art* in general is widely regarded as an indicator that the person concerned can look forward to a period of happiness and financial stability. In some countries, Britain, America, and Australia in particular, the dream is also believed to indicate an inheritance, or at least some financial benefit, is on the way. The Chinese also maintain that to dream of selling antiques presages a time when it is not wise to lend or borrow money.

ANTS
Dreams about ants have been recorded in the Far East for many centuries. By general consensus they mean that the dreamer may expect an unsettled period when he or she will spend a lot of time chasing little worries and finding small annoyances in many day-to-day activities. Some writers have claimed that this is only really true if the ants were actually seen on clothing or in food. To see ants busy on their ceaseless activities is, according to South American dream lore, a sign that a change in life direction, such as a new job or moving home, would bring happiness and satisfaction. Recent American sources have claimed that any dream of ants is symbolic of good business activities.

APPLES
Apples in dreams have always been regarded as good omens throughout Britain and Europe. It does not really matter whether the apples are seen individually or in large

numbers on trees, the old almanacs insist such visions point to a period when hopes can be realised and endeavour will be rewarded. Only large numbers of apples seen decaying on the ground are said to serve as a warning against undertaking schemes that are too ambitious for they are in danger of failure. In America, a dream of eating a sweet apple points to a happy event, while a sour apple indicates an unexpected problem.

ARCH

The arch was a familiar symbol in Roman dream lore and was believed to symbolise a rise in society, unless the arch was broken or damaged in any way in which case the omens foretold a setback in plans. In Europe, the arch was said to represent wealth and advancement, though to dream of passing under one was a warning that people would come seeking favours. Several Victorian almanacs mention that the young girl who dreamed of a fallen arch was in for an unhappy period in her love-life. Modern sources suggest the dream of an arch signifies that whatever efforts the sleeper is making towards specific objectives, are in the right direction.

ARMY

Dreams about armies, or soldiers in general, have been much studied since the time of the ancient Romans. The earliest writers believed these night visions had nothing to do with fighting but were a sign that the dreamer would shortly be faced with a number of obstacles to overcome before achieving his or her aims in life. If the soldiers were seen on the march then this suggested the dreamer would have to travel to succeed in his plans. For many years almanacs have also reported that to dream of wounded soldiers is an omen of misfortune; while an unmarried woman who sees members of the armed forces is being warned against becoming involved in casual love-affairs. Several American sources have also stated that dreams of the army symbolise 'war in the family', although to see one's own national army foretells business success.

ATTICS
Attics have become increasingly commonplace elements in dreams, and since the seventeenth century have been seen as symbolising vain hopes. In Europe, for a man to imagine being in an attic is a sign that his ambitions will be frustrated, while a woman will find her love-life disappointing. A nineteenth-century American almanac was rather more encouraging, informing any dreamer who saw themself in an attic that they would, eventually, escape from their 'clutter of problems'. Some modern authorities have suggested that the dream is actually a warning to the young against promiscuity, but, in contrast, a comfort to older people by implying that their advancing years are going to be peaceful and happy.

AVALANCHE
The avalanche has had a place in dream lore for several centuries, particularly in Europe, where it is regarded as a rather ominous symbol of formidable objects facing the dreamer. These troubles will certainly require changes in plans to overcome. Conversely, though, the almanacs and dream books of France, Germany and Switzerland are all agreed that to dream of being buried in an avalanche of snow is a sign of getting some spectacular good luck! In America, to merely *witness* an avalanche signifies good fortune. A recent British authority has suggested the dream indicates that the subject is taking a negative attitude towards life and should be much more positive.

B

BABY

Babies are referred to in the earliest documents about dreaming, the oracles stating that the woman who dreamed of a baby would soon become pregnant. The Greeks, however, were the first to decide that the dreams did not necessarily relate to infants, claiming that to imagine a baby suckling milk from a mother's breast indicated pleasure in life, while the baby suckling from a wet nurse was an omen of sickness. By the Middle Ages, a happy baby was said to be symbolic of enjoying good friendships, while any dream in which an infant took its first steps was a clear hint about making firm decisions concerning the future. European sources also believe that to dream of nursing a baby is a warning about being deceived by a trusted friend.

BAGS

Baggage has been described as symbolic of travel and prosperity, although empty bags point to financial problems. In earlier times, to dream of a baggage train prophesied a long journey, and if the bags were being carried by others then the dreamer could expect a change of fortune for the better. Curiously, several Victorian almanacs claimed that to lose a bag indicated coming into some money, but to imagine other people's baggage was a bad omen for love-affairs.

American books of dream lore have also said that to see baggage inside a house or a building is a sign that a trip is about to be cancelled.

BAKING
The baking of bread or cakes has featured in dream lore since biblical times. According to many authorities, it is a dream of contrary for women prophesying times of hardship, although for a man it is a sign of coming into money. A single woman who dreamed of baking was also warned she could lose her friends because of her bad temper. The bakehouse or bakery is mentioned in several European almanacs as being a warning against making a change of occupation, although the young woman who dreams of working in one is in danger of seduction. Modern researchers believe the dream is symbolic of a concern about future prosperity, and in the case of parents a particular worry about the needs of their children.

BALDNESS
To dream of going bald is a warning of ill health, according to all the authorities, although for many generations the dreamer who imagines going completely bald is going to be loved passionately. Since the Middle Ages, for a man to dream of a bald-headed male has been a sign to be on guard against deception, while if he dreams of a bald-headed woman he will have an argumentative wife. The woman who dreams of a bald-headed man will apparently have difficulties in her love-life.

BALLET
Since the great Romantic era of ballet in the early part of the nineteenth century, this art has become a familiar feature in dream research, though the omens are only said to be really good if the dreamer is dancing. The first mention in European almanacs claims that the dream signifies infidelity to a woman and business problems for a man. Several Victorian

books of dream lore state that to imagine watching a professional performance foreshadows poor health, and
modern research has tended to confirm this conviction,
believing the dream signifies a need to take more exercise
and allow the mind to relax from everyday problems.

BANK

The dreamer who finds himself in a bank is being guided
not only about his finances but also his future. To witness
coins and banknotes being handed in, counted or accumulated is an omen that the dreamer will prosper and earn
widespread respect. Money being handed out to others is a
warning against carelessness, while if it is being given
directly to the dreamer then this is an indicator to expect
some good luck. A deserted bank foretells business losses.
In several recent dream almanacs it has been suggested that
to dream of becoming bankrupt is both a warning against
speculation and at the same time an omen of financial gain!
At their most basic, dreams about banking are reflective of
worries over money matters.

BANQUET

The Latin Americans have a strong tradition about dreams
which feature banquets. The more lavish the setting, the
wealthier-looking the guests, and the more sumptuous the
meal — the better the omens. A great banquet points to
happiness and contentment in the dreamer's family while
friends and acquaintances will be happy to perform
favours. The only warning signs are any empty places at
the tables or strange-looking guests; these are warnings of
misunderstandings or disappointments that loom in the
future. In Europe, empty places at a big dinner are said to
be a caution to the dreamer to curb a tendency to quarrel
with family or friends.

BAPTISM

Being an eyewitness to a baptism in a dream has been a

topic much discussed in religious works. Its significance in most of these has been seen as a warning that the dreamer's character needs strengthening, and that he or she should desist from 'some lustful engagement' to quote one seventeenth-century German authority, 'Or else be thrown into a state of terror over being discovered'. A broader interpretation says the baptism dream is an omen of unforeseen circumstances adversely affecting the future, though there is a promise of better times around the corner.

BARBECUE
Dreams of barbecues or picnics are indicators of happy times ahead, especially for the young. In America, the dreams are qualified by the prevailing conditions such as the weather or the mood of the guests. Any signs of rain or discord among the people are read as a temporary set-back in business affairs or matters of the heart. Another recent definition has suggested that if the sleeper sees a whole animal being roasted on the barbecue then some relatives or friends are about to impose themselves on the household!

BATHING
Bathing was associated in dream lore with a desire for purification in the earliest times. The authorities believed the images did not represent a desire for physical cleanliness but an effort to attain forgiveness for some transgression — which could well explain why it is now believed that a hot bath signifies evil and a cold one good health. Several nineteenth-century almanacs take this further by stating that pregnant women who dream of hot baths risk a miscarriage, while a man may commit adultery! A bath in which the water appeared murky was also a warning of health problems. Twentieth-century rationalisation of these dreams has turned the omens on their heads: a warm bath promises the realisation of long held plans, while a cold one cautions against acting hastily in any scheme

under consideration. The general act of taking a bath can also reveal a growing sexual interest in a member of the opposite sex, an American source has added.

BATTLE
The oldest existing documents of the ancient Egyptians mention dreams of battle which were taken as literal prophesies of conflict to come. The Roman oracles, however, felt the dreams could have more personal application: a battle on land being a warning about business transactions, and one at sea on problems in affairs of the heart. By the Middle Ages, to be on the triumphant side in any battle was an omen of good fortune, while to be defeated indicated that other people would spoil the dreamer's prospects. Victorian almanacs claimed it was a very good sign to dream of fighting a battle alone as this would lead to a resolution of some current problem. A consensus of modern opinions says that the dream is a warning about some deep-seated grievance against another person, which needs to be brought into the open.

BEACH
Though it is only in comparatively recent times that mankind has used beaches purely as somewhere for relaxation and swimming, they have featured in dream lore since before the times of the ancient Greeks. The earliest images were much concerned with the breaking of waves on the shore, said to represent the rhythm of existence: the height and sweep of the breakers signifying the duration and tranquillity of the dreamer's life. In time, too, with the association of the waves with 'white horses', these came to be read in dreams as omens of suppressed emotions. Later European authorities have also stated that dreams of walking along a beach foretell that financial aid is shortly going to be required by the dreamer. An interesting explanation of these prognostications for what should be a

happy dream, is that sand has always been considered a symbol of famine and loss.

BEDROOM
To dream of a bedroom is an omen of change, and to see one that has recently been refurnished also promises some happy experiences in the future. Several old English almanacs maintain that to dream of being in a bed in a strange room signifies a visit from some unexpected friends or an improvement in business matters, while a woman who dreams of making a bed will soon have a new occupation — or lover. For centuries it was thought a bad sign for a sick person to dream of being in bed as this could lead to further complications. The Russians believed that to see bedbugs was a sign of continuing illness, possibly death, in a family — unless the dreamer was able to get rid of the unpleasant insects. To dream of being in bed with someone you have never met before is an omen of being unreasonably distrustful of those with whom you come into contact. Recently, American sources have suggested that any dream of a bedroom, or a bed, is symbolic of worries and fears in the dreamer's mind about his or her sex life.

BEES
Bees are symbolic of happiness and success, and since time immemorial they have been regarded as very happy omens in dreams. Rural almanacs published wherever bees are kept claim they indicate good business transactions, especially if they are seen flying around the hive, although to be stung by them in a dream will result in a reversal of some kind. American authorities have stated that to watch bees making honey, points to financial gains, and like other sources on this side of the Atlantic are convinced that to kill or injure bees will result in losing some good friends.

BEGGAR
Since the Middle Ages dreams about beggars have been

regarded as instances of contrary: to see a beggar will result in receiving some unexpected help, while to imagine being one signifies an improvement in finances. Some Victorian dream books, however, took a strongly moralistic tone on such dreams, reporting that to meet a beggar was a sign of bad management demanding immediate economies, while to make a gift to one denoted 'dissatisfaction with present surroundings'. A recent American almanac has claimed that to dream of giving money to someone begging means that a new love-affair will be reciprocated. A similar British source maintains that the dream is symbolic of being ashamed to ask for help with some pressing problems.

BIRDS
Dreams of birds have been the subject of much debate among authorities. Many of the earlier oracles believed they symbolised a desire to be free, while later writers, including Freud, have associated them with love and passion. The Greeks and Romans claimed that the larger the bird in the dream, the higher a person might hope to aspire; while particularly colourful birds signified a bright future. By the Middle Ages, the young girl who dreamed of a bird with beautiful plumage would soon find a suitable partner, while to imagine catching a bird was a premonition of a wedding. Caged birds, however, were later said by European sources to point to marital rows, and dead birds forecast sadness and disappointment in love-affairs. Freud has claimed that the bird is actually a phallic symbol and to dream about the creature on the wing reveals a burning desire to be good at sex.

BLEEDING
Bleeding has been a feature in dreams for centuries, and some of the old almanacs consider blood to be very ill-omened. At best, such a dream was a sign that fortune was turning against the dreamer, while at worst it signified malicious reports about a person were being circulated

which could well end in his or her death. To see blood-stained garments is a warning to watch out for rivals who would ruin a successful career, while blood on the dreamer's hands is said to be a sign of poor health. The most widely proffered advice after a dream of blood is to avoid controversy with family or friends.

BOATS
Although boats in dreams are today generally recognised as symbols of a person's life, the ancient Arabic dream books related all maritime expeditions to danger and illusion and believed these night visions alluded to adventures with women! The Roman oracles, however, claimed it was the circumstances in which the vessel was seen that governed the omens, stating that to dream of steering a boat skilfully was a good omen; though if the waters turned rough then some unhappy changes in life could be expected. European sources in the seventeenth century reported that the man who dreamed of being shipwrecked was about to be betrayed by a woman, while for a woman to see a fleet of small boats pointed to a very happy social life. A recent American source has added that anyone who dreams of falling overboard from a boat will have a narrow escape from death — probably an echo of the ancient tradition of committing the dead to the sea in small boats.

BOOKS
Considering the important part they play in our lives, books have apparently not featured a great deal in dream lore. A writer in the late seventeenth century declared that to dream of old books was a warning to shun evil in any form; while a Parisian antiquarian in the last century said that dreams about great libraries were a good omen for anyone involved in creative or artistic pursuits. More recently, it has been claimed that to dream of visiting a library or bookstore is a sign of literary aspirations; but if any of the shelves happen to be empty the dreamer's

talents may be limited. In general, to dream of books is
an omen of a happy, calm, if not spectacularly successful
life.

BORROWING
Dreams in which the act of borrowing occurs can be read in
one of two ways. Both European and American authorities
believe instances where the dreamer finds himself borrowing are an indication of imminent loss, possibly of money,
but more likely of friends. While on the other hand if the
dreamer is being asked to loan something to another
person he may expect help from friends when faced with a
similar situation. The Italians also believe such dreams are a
warning against over-generosity.

BOXES
Many a dream has been reported in which boxes have been
seen, but in a large number of these, the dreamers can
never be quite sure what was in the box, or indeed if
anything was in it at all! Therein lies the clue to the omen of
the dream. An empty box is, not surprisingly, said to
signify a failure of some kind in the dreamer's life, while
a full box promises travel in the near future. If specific items
are seen in the box, consult the appropriate entry in this
book for an explanation — though money or any other
object of value may be taken as a general indication of good
fortune.

BREASTS
To dream of breasts has been considered a good omen since
the time of the ancient Greeks. The men and women of this
early civilisation believed that the larger the breasts the
better the omen, and that full, white breasts were a sign of
monetary wealth. In Europe, since the Middle Ages, any
woman who dreamed of suckling an infant at her breast
could expect a happy event — not necessarily childbirth;

30

while a man who saw himself resting his head on a woman's bosom was about to begin a new and important friendship. Several dream almanacs also state that a woman who dreams of a brassière will soon increase her circle of friends. Perhaps, though, the most curious dream interpretation in this category is to be found in a nine-teenth-century English manual which warns young ladies, 'If a lover is slyly observing it (her bosom) through her sheer corsage, she is about to come under the soft, persuasive influence of a too ardent wooer.'

BRIDGE

Crossing bridges while asleep is another very ancient dream. Some of the oldest records document stories of dreamers being faced by seemingly endless bridges which disappear into darkness and which no amount of effort can surmount. Such dreams are believed to be omens of loss and problems lying ahead. If the bridge appears to be in a poor state of repair — even on the point of collapse — then German sources advise watching out for false promises from friends or associates. The French suggest lovers should take this as an indication that their partner will fail to live up to expectations. Only a dream in which the bridge is viewed in daylight and is successfully crossed without incident, promises happy times ahead.

BROTHER

Greek sources first stated that to dream of a brother had different interpretations for the other brothers or sisters. The woman who dreamed of her brother could look forward to domestic happiness, but for a man to think of his brother foretold a family argument. In the Middle Ages, to dream of a brother dying was a curiously good omen for it meant the downfall of enemies. Late nineteenth-century almanacs claimed that any dream of brothers and sisters being together harmoniously, indicated financial security.

Recent research has suggested that any dream of a brother is a subconscious message the dreamer is neglecting his or her family.

BUILDINGS
Dreams in which clearly discernible buildings feature are generally good omens. For several centuries in Europe to dream of a large house surrounded by rolling, well-cared for land has been a sign of a long life and much travel. Small, modern houses are an omen of a happy home life, while any building that is old and has been allowed to fall into disrepair is a pointer to ill-health and personal misfortune. Experts are agreed that buildings in dreams are a representation of the dreamer's achievements and attitudes towards life, and to ignore the significance of them is ill-advised.

BURGLAR
Dreams of thieves breaking into homes are several centuries old and were first defined as a warning about having dangerous enemies to contend with. The Victorians, however, believed them to be symbolic of a person's business or social reputation which was in danger of being damaged through carelessness. Some recent authorities have suggested that this may actually be a dream of contrary: to imagine being burgled will lead to an increase of worldly goods; although others feel it should be read as a much simpler message to take greater care of possessions.

BURIED ALIVE
An often frightening dream which most authorities are agreed is a warning against any dishonourable act. Eighteenth-century European almanacs believed the dream foretold making a major error of judgement which enemies would use to destroy the dreamer; while in the Far East it was said to be a good omen to see others being buried alive as this signified wealth and power. Although some more

recent American sources have suggested to dream of being incarcerated in this way could be another case of contrary forecasting a rise to fame — a more widely held conclusion is that it is symbolic of a need for change and a move away from bad influences which are threatening to overwhelm the dreamer.

C

CABIN

The first records of dreams about ships' cabins being places of ill-omen are to be found in sixteenth-century documents. Although the cabin may have been a haven from storms while at sea, in dream lore it was said to be symbolic of 'trouble brewing'. Two centuries later, a dream of being locked in a cabin indicated ill-health — according to several European almanacs — while if there was a member of the opposite sex present then the dreamer was hiding a guilty secret. The Victorian books of dream lore all agreed the dream symbolised domestic upheavals. Modern research, however, has also suggested this dream is a warning against becoming careless and to put more effort into life.

CALL

Dreams in which the voice of a dead ancestor is heard are among the most eerie on record. Such calls are said to contain a warning about the dreamer's health, and a nineteenth-century almanac explains them thus: 'The voice is an echo thrown back from the future on the subjective mind ... a certain portion of mind matter remains the same in lines of family descent.' In more general terms, to hear a call in a dream is an omen of some important message, while if the voice is identifiable as a member of the family or a friend then it presages misfortune, perhaps sickness, among

34

those nearest and dearest. A number of strange voices calling denote troubles in business life.

CAMPING
To dream of camping in the open air is a happy omen of a change in affairs. If the vision was of a holiday camp then expect to change jobs; while if it was a camping settlement, such as a caravan park, then a family known to the dreamer is about to move home. To camp under canvas is rather inauspicious for it indicates that a long and difficult journey lies ahead. All these interpretations are of British origin; the Spanish believe a woman who dreams of seeing a military camp will be unfaithful to her husband, while the Germans say that any female who dreams of being among soldiers in camp will marry the first time she has the chance.

CANCER
The fear of having cancer has been the subject of an increasing number of dreams, according to reports from American medical authorities. Dream experts, however, believe this is another dream of contrary, and not a sign the dreamer has, or will contract, the illness. To imagine getting it is said to presage settling quarrels with loved ones; while to be cured of it indicates a welcome rise in a person's finances. There is still an element of warning about the dream, however, and that is the dreamer should not take risks with his or her health.

CANDLES
Phallic interpretations have been offered for years about dreams in which candles appear, the majority of these having originated from the popular seventeenth-century definition that a maiden who dreamed of moulding candles would soon find herself a vigorous lover. At this same period of history, a girl who dreamed of lighting a candle was also believed to be on the verge of an affair in which she would have to meet her lover clandestinely, because of

objections by her parents. Conversely, since before the Middle Ages, a brightly shining candle has been described in most books of dream lore as an omen of contentment and good relationships with family and friends. To see a candle guttering·is a sign of new opportunities, while any dream in which a lighted candlestick appears, points to a bright future with health, happiness and loving companions.

CAR
'The car of your dreams' is a favourite advertising slogan, but to imagine one in your sleep is no guarantee of owning the latest model. Indeed, most experts are agreed there is no particular omen attached to such a dream — unless the car is speeding, breaks down or has an accident. The first indicates some unexpected news is on the way; the second that an embarrassing situation is looming; and the third that an item which was lost will shortly be unexpectedly found. Nothing very mechanical about any of those! Finally, in any dream where the sleeper imagines himself at the wheel of a car and drives safely through several hazards, is about to have a long-held ambition realised.

CASTLES
Castles are an omen of travel and of meeting people of many different nations. Some earlier books of dream lore maintain castles are also a sign of wealth, and that anyone who dreams regularly about them is a romantic by nature and should take the greatest care when selecting a partner for life. A French almanac, reprinted numerous times since the sixteenth century, states that anyone who dreams of leaving a castle, where they have apparently lived for some time, will lose a lover or experience the bereavement of someone close. Modern authorities have also suggested that the castle is symbolic of imprisonment, and the dreamer should try to escape by opening his or her mind to new influences.

CATS

To dream about cats is generally considered an omen of misfortune, though that may well be hard for feline lovers to accept. A cat that spits or attacks is a sign there are people trying to blacken the dreamer's character, but the bad luck would have been avoided if the animal was driven away. An English almanac says a dream about a scraggy cat is an indication that a friend has fallen ill, while a clean, white cat is a sign of impending entanglements with the opposite sex which could lead to unhappiness. The French claim that a young girl who dreams of cuddling a cat is likely to be easily seduced; while the Italians say a man who sees himself being scratched by a cat will suffer losses in his business dealings.

CATTLE

The rural almanacs of America indicate a long tradition of dream lore associated with cattle, much of which, though, is undeniably European in origin. Most of the omens are good, with those featuring large, healthy herds grazing contentedly the most auspicious for prosperity and happiness. Americans believe that a stampeding herd of cattle indicates the dreamer will have to use all his powers of command to succeed in business; while to see a lot of calves points to good profits from forthcoming deals. In Britain, calves are said to signify improved social standing for a man and a faithful lover for a woman. The French claim that weak and shaggy-looking cattle indicate a life of toil and struggle, but to dream of cattle being milked is a sign of good fortune in store.

CAVE

To dream of being in a cave from which there is apparently no exit, is another widely quoted dream and one which signifies increased problems in the dreamer's life. The Chinese called a cavity a maternal symbol, and yet said that merely to see the entrance to a cave, by night, was a harbinger of threat to both health and work. In Britain, it is known as an obstacle dream, and there is a word of cheer for those who find their way out of the cave before waking — their problems will be solved in time. The Germans believe the cave dream foreshadows change in a person's life with possible estrangement from some members of the family. A nineteenth-century Italian dream book for lovers claims that a young girl who dreams of walking into a cave with her lover will end up marrying someone totally unsuitable! Some modern sources also believe this dream is symbolic of being trapped in an unsuitable way of life and every effort should be made to get out of it.

CELLAR
Like the cave dream, to find oneself in a cold and dank cellar does not bode well for the future. In particular, it denotes a loss of confidence — even a loss of property — without the strongest application of willpower against these eventualities. The dreamer who feels trapped in the cellar is being warned about failing to meet commitments which could result in losing some good friends. The French, in particular, believe that a cellar seen well-stocked with wines or foodstuffs indicates a profitable future. But any young girl finding herself in this situation should beware the smooth tongue of a man who will shortly thereafter offer marriage ... because he will prove to be a compulsive gambler!

CEMETERY
The omens of dreams about a cemetery are not as bad as might be expected, for they symbolise not death, but an attachment to the past. Indeed, there are several old books of dream lore that maintain it means the dreamer will receive unexpected news about someone they thought was dead. In general, a tidy and well looked after cemetery is a pointer to future prosperity, particularly if children are seen in the vicinity. A neglected cemetery is a warning to take care of personal and business affairs or run the risk of

serious disruption to life. An English almanac adds that for a woman to dream of taking flowers to a cemetery is a cheering sign she can expect good health for her family.

CHAINS
Chains have been an uneasy omen in dreams since the time of the Roman Empire, when they were seen as symbolic of worries and difficulty. To dream of being bound in chains was said to presage many unjust burdens which could only be removed by breaking the links. In the Middle Ages to dream of others in chains was a warning to be on guard against the machinations of enemies. Eighteenth-century almanacs claimed that to imagine a woman wearing a gold chain around her neck was a good sign for love-affairs. Modern research has also suggested this dream is symbolic of marriage problems which the dreamer will have to work at resolving.

CHEATING
Cheating is an element that has been noted in a surprisingly large number of dreams, and the consensus of opinion is that to be cheated, is an omen the dreamer may shortly expect some good luck! Some of the oldest almanacs speak of cheating as being a warning against dubious dealing in business, though all are agreed that if the dreamer is doing the cheating he or she is about to be caught out. A Spanish book of dream lore claims that for young people to imagine themselves being cheated at games, foretells the loss of a lover through quarrels and misunderstandings.

CHEESE
'Eating cheese at night causes bad dreams' is a familiar expression, but in actual fact dreams of this tasty food are said to be symbolic of health and happiness. Records from the sixteenth century indicate that to dream of making cheese indicated success in business ventures, and not long after this, almanacs were claiming that for a young man or

woman to imagine eating cheese pointed to a satisfying love-affair. In Europe, dreams of cheese are said to indicate the dreamer likes only the best things; although, in America, smelly cheeses are believed to predict social embarrassment. A very down-to-earth British source stated recently that any dream of cheese was a suggestion the dreamer needed more protein.

CHICKENS
Chickens are a familiar creature in dreams according to several old country almanacs, but not necessarily good omens. Chickens seen roosting are a sign that someone is nursing a grudge against you, while a brood of restless chickens indicate a number of problems gathering on the horizon. Only young chicks bode well for future plans, though considerable energy will have to be expanded to make these schemes work. One nineteenth-century book of folk lore warns about a dream of eating chickens, as this, it says, is a sign of selfishness which will adversely affect the dreamer's love-life and business affairs. American sources, however, are more positive about chickens, claiming the birds are symbolic of friendship, fertility and a good love-life.

CHILDREN
Many dreams about children have been cited for their accuracy, though the omens vary curiously with the health of the youngsters. Children at play are a sign of happiness and prosperity, while miserable little folk are an indication of worry and disappointment. For a mother to dream that her child has a minor ailment is actually a sign the youngster will enjoy robust health, while for any parent to see a dead child should be taken as a serious warning of ill-health in the family. The best-omened dream of all is to imagine being involved with children in their games. A recent British source has suggested that dreams about children could

be a repressed desire for a family or a longing for childhood again.

CHURCH
The omens about churches are mixed. To see a gloomy church from a distance will presage a disappointment in some long-held plans, while to actually enter the building means the dreamer will soon be participating in a funeral. According to several European almanacs, for a young girl to dream of her fiancé entering a church before their wedding day can signify the marriage will never take place, or alternatively warn that the union will be unhappy. To dream of walking through a churchyard on a pleasant day, and into a church, is an omen of visiting some enjoyable places and making new friends. According to a recent American dream book to see ministers or priests 'signifies unsurpassed lust and ambition' predicting dishonour and unhappiness in store for the dreamer.

CIRCUS
Visiting a circus is exciting in itself but to dream about one promises more excitement and fun in the dreamer's life. A number of sources also say it presages a visit from an old friend, and if children are in the dream, too, then this is a sign of some financial luck. The only warning note about such a dream is to be careful of the impression you give to others at social functions.

CLIMBING
Authorities are agreed that any dream of climbing is a projection. of the person's deepest ambitions, and the tougher the test faced in the climb the harder the dreamer will need to strive to achieve those goals. To reach the summit of a mountain has long been believed to signify a prosperous future, while climbing a ladder or stairs to the top predicts success in business. To receive any kind of assistance while climbing indicates the dreamer will need

41

the support of friends to succeed, though to fall or fail to reach the top of any obstacle, points to real problems ahead. Should an actual climber have this dream, some experts advise caution in case it could be a psychic warning.

CLOTHING
An analysis of the type and condition of clothes seen in the dream is important in defining its meaning, according to most books of dream lore. New clothes are predictably an omen of good fortune, while old and ragged clothes are a bad sign for both business and love-affairs. Curiously, several European almanacs insist that dreamers who see themselves wearing a lot of clothes should prepare for hard times ahead, and vice versa. Taking off clothes in a dream, however, is an omen of good fortune, and a recent French dream book says that seeing clothes on back-to-front, or wearing clothes that are too tight, is a warning against excess sexual activity.

CLOUDS
Clouds are symbolic of something intermediary, according to recent research into dreams, although, since the days of the earliest civilisations, the types of clouds seen in dreams have been read as portents. Dark, heavy clouds predict misfortune and bad management, and accompanied by rain the signs are even grimmer, with sickness and family problems threatened. White clouds in a clear sky point to happy times ahead, especially in dealings with the opposite sex. A blanket of grey clouds is a sign that the dreamer is creating undue difficulties which are preventing his or her advancement in life.

COFFEE
For a time, dreams of coffee were considered ill-omened. One notorious American almanac of the 1880s suggested it implied domestic upheaval for married couples and sexual promiscuity for young girls. However, the twentieth

century has seen these ideas replaced. Nowadays, to dream of drinking a good cup of coffee is an omen of good news, while to grind the beans is a sign of happy relationships with family and friends. The only thing that is not so good is to have spilled the coffee, for this presages a few small problems.

COFFIN
Since the Middle Ages a dream of a coffin has been generally regarded as a good omen, and for the dreamer to actually see themself in the coffin spells out a long life and happiness. Although in the intervening years a few European almanacs have described coffins as symbolising debts, illness and sorrow, the consensus of opinion says this is another dream of contrary: far from predicting somebody will die it is more likely to presage good news such as an inheritance. Some American sources believe it could even indicate a wedding, while recent research has concluded it is more likely to be symbolising the end of one part of the dreamer's life and the beginning of a new and more exciting period.

CONCERT
German and Austrian books of dream lore have for many years placed a special importance on dreams featuring concerts. Apart from being an omen of pleasure to come, they are also said to be a signal to the overworked person to use music for relaxation. British and American sources maintain that good news will follow such a dream, unless the music was discordant or interrupted in any way — then a short illness is being forecast. In some of the older almanacs a dream of a concert is listed as being a portent for businessmen of successful trading in the offing.

CONE
The cone shape is another phallic symbol and has been described by every dream interpreter from Ptolemy

onwards as representing a desire for exceptional sexual pleasure. Some of the Victorian books of dream lore skirted such a direct interpretation by claiming that a dream about anything cone-shaped, such as an icing funnel or a measuring glass, would 'ensure the blushing maiden a happy marriage and the young man a beautiful bride'.

COOKING
The act of cooking in a dream presages some good news, including visits from a number of friends. In some European dream books it is said that a young girl who dreams of cooking will shortly afterwards become engaged, while a man who sees himself busy at this activity is about to be invited to a party. Some older English sources claim that a woman who visualises herself cooking is facing possible divorce and poverty. Of late, the omen has, happily, been revised to signify a period of material comfort.

CORNFIELDS
Since the dawn of human history, corn has been looked upon as a fertility symbol and in dream lore it is similarly regarded as an omen of prosperity and fulfilment. Many almanacs describe the sight of growing corn as signifying monetary benefit, especially if the ears are large. If the corn is being harvested in the dream then good news is on the way, while to eat a stalk of corn presages a happy union with a member of the opposite sex.

COTTAGE
Dreams of a cottage in the country are as likely to occur during busy waking hours as they are by night, and in either case indicate a weariness with everyday toil and a longing for the simple life. To dream of a cottage signifies better times ahead, though most authorities agree that to see other people in a cottage is merely a forerunner of good news. An empty cottage, though, is not a welcome insight because it points to loneliness and trouble for the dreamer.

COUNTRYSIDE

This is a dream of contrary in which thoughts of escaping to the countryside are said to be an omen of losing your home. The Americans have a strong tradition that to see the countryside by night, in a dream, is a sign of illness and melancholy, and if the landscape is dry and bare then troubled times lie ahead. In Europe, for a man to dream of inheriting a piece of property is an omen of gaining a beautiful wife; while for a woman to dream of spending time in the country signifies a long journey — though not necessarily to the country!

COURT CASE

Medical records show that dreams of appearing in court are very common. They should, indeed, be treated with respect for they are forewarnings of financial problems; with a secondary message that someone may well be trying to deceive you. Several American authorities believe that a dream of going to court points to business losses, while to imagine being sentenced indicates travel and prosperity! A general consensus of opinion suggests this particular dream is urging more consideration for others in order to avoid serious troubles in the future.

CRASH

The crash dream can be vivid and startling, waking the dreamer in an instant, yet according to most authorities it should be regarded as an omen of important achievements. The crash can occur in a train, a car or an aeroplane, and the more dramatic the setting, the better the achievement will prove to be. To be a witness to a collision between vehicles, however, is a warning to the dreamer that it is time to make a decision with regard to some crucial matter in his or her life. In Europe, for a young woman to see a collision denotes that she will have two lovers and find it difficult to choose between them.

CROW

The crow is a frequent symbol in dreams and associated almost wholly with misfortune. Yet when the bird appeared over the fields of the first agricultural peoples, he was seen as a sign of prosperity and civilisation. With the passage of time and the awareness of his pillaging of seeds and crops, he has become the bird of death. To see a crow in a dream is now an omen of grief and misfortune, and a flock flying overhead signify a death in the family. A British almanac further adds that to hear the cawing of crows in a dream presages illness in children, while to a young man 'it is indicative of his succumbing to the wiles of designing women'.

CURTAINS

A dream of curtains can often be extremely frustrating as the dreamer never quite manages to get through them. For generations, in fact, curtains have been accepted as symbolising a warning about the future, and the dreamer would be well advised to mend his ways before they are opened. Several almanacs declare that to dream of curtains foretells the arrival of unwelcome visitors, while the sight of torn and dirty curtains is a sign of quarrelling in the family.

D

DANCING

Dreams of dancing are recorded by the ancient Greeks who believed them to be symbolic of joy and happiness. It was a particularly good omen to see children and young people dancing as this pointed to a happy home life. By the Middle Ages, the sight of people dancing was said to indicate good news of absent friends, while those who imagined themselves dancing, very gracefully, would succeed in all their plans. In the eighteenth century, young lovers who dreamed of dancing together were told their love would be accepted by their parents. The Victorian books of dream lore claimed that the young woman who dreamed of dancing at a ball with handsome young men would find an excellent husband — an omen repeated in many similar modern volumes. Recent studies have stated the dream symbolises a desire for more pleasure to 'dance the blues away'.

DANGER

Danger can manifest itself in many forms in a dream, but taken in general terms it is agreed by the authorities that the omens are the opposite to what might be expected. In other words, where the dreamer finds himself in a dangerous place or situation it is a pointer to success and honour in life — though he should never scorn the help of friends.

Ptolemy recorded this dream, and remarked that it was essential for the subject to have faced up to the danger in order to achieve success. Some modern writers have advised taking such night visions as a warning of real danger lying ahead; and if the threat was physical, to be especially careful in matters of health.

DARK
To dream of being in a dark place or alone somewhere on a dark night is ill-omened and indicates difficulties lying ahead, perhaps because the dreamer has been ignoring good advice. Some of the oldest books of dreams mention falling or stumbling in the dark as a sign to expect changes for the worst; and to encounter other people in this situation is a further presentiment of loneliness and trouble. According to European sources, a dream of walking in the dark points to the recovery of some lost item such as money; while if you lose someone, such as a friend or a child in the darkness, then a period of anxiety in both home and business life will follow.

DAUGHTER
Victorian dream books contain lengthy references to dreams about daughters. The consensus of opinion being that for a parent to dream of a daughter is a sign that, no matter what displeasing events may be taking place in the home at the time, they will soon be followed by harmony and contentment. Some other sources, notably European, are not so optimistic. The Germans believe a dream of talking to a daughter is a forewarning of emotional sorrow, while the French claim that to dream of an adopted daughter presages serious trouble ahead. A curious Italian almanac adds that when a mother dreams about her only daughter she will shortly afterwards become pregnant!

DEAF
A curious experience in which the dreamer appears to be

deaf or unable to make contact with anyone else in the dream because they, too, cannot hear. Nonetheless, the omens are far from unhappy ones, because to dream of being deaf indicates financial success, while if the other people could not hear, then a number of worrying problems are about to be solved. An American source claims that to imagine suddenly becoming deaf, points to an equally sudden promotion.

DEATH

Dreams of death are among the oldest on record, and have been held in especial regard by leading authorities such as Paracelsus who wrote, 'It may happen that the soul of persons who have died, perhaps 50 years ago, may appear to us in a dream and we should pay attention for such a vision is not an illusion or delusion.' Nor are the omens bad, for this is a classic dream of contrary: a vision of death signifies good news. If the dreamer is the dead person, then a release from worries or illness can be expected, while if it was someone else then an inheritance is forthcoming. Dream books in the Middle Ages list seeing a dead body as indicating that a wedding will take place; observing the death of an enemy as news of a birth; and talking to a dead person as a pointer to a long life. Perhaps the most bizarre dream in this category concerns seeing a dead person lying in a coffin, for this, says an American almanac, is a sign of suffering from indigestion.

DEBTS

Another widely recorded dream which poses the question: has the dreamer let anybody down recently, or does someone owe him money? To be repaying a debt indicates a beneficial event to come, while to have a debt repaid is a sign the dreamer can expect a loss. According to an American almanac, any dreamer who imagines being determined not to pay a debt had better expect some very serious problems in his or her personal life.

DECORATING

To dream of decorating a house or flat is certainly regarded by European authorities as indicating a happy period of life ahead; but in America, to do one's own decorating presages losses either in business, or of friends. Decorating windows, though, is universally agreed to herald changes for the better; though to be watched at this activity by others is, curiously, a sign that however talented the dreamer may be, few will recognise his or her ability.

DEER

Deer have been omens of good luck for centuries, and to dream of a herd indicates great friendships. According to British sources, a single deer presages good news, while several deer on the run means the news will be about money. A captive deer warns of unhappiness, and though for centuries it was held that the death of a deer would result in an inheritance, more recent evidence suggests it is indicating the use of caution in dealing with supposed friends.

DEFORMED

Psychiatric records indicate that a considerable number of people have dreams of being deformed in some way, and that this is by no means a new phenomenon. Old documents from the Middle Ages reveal that images of being a cripple were regarded as a portent of hunger and distress in a family; while in the Victorian era such visions were understood to be foretelling of an appeal from relatives or friends, which it was best not to refuse. Modern authorities speak of it as a sign the dreamer may need help to 'straighten out' his or her life, though in general terms it augurs small family disagreements. According to an American source, to see other people as deformed is a caution to guard against false appearances in others.

DESERT

Desert landscapes are another recurring image in dreams and have long been accepted as foreshadowing troubles ahead. To imagine struggling across a desert points to difficulties with important plans; while if the weather turns into a sandstorm there is a danger of being let down by friends. A number of modern sources suggest that the desert symbolises a desperate need for sympathy and understanding. The dreamer who imagines dying of thirst in a desert is actually having difficulty coping with the stresses of everyday life and should seek help.

DEVIL

The Devil figure appearing in a variety of disguises has long been part of dream lore, but there is very little consistency in the omens of such dreams. A Victorian almanac, for example, says, 'Beware of associating with the Devil — even in dreams — for he is always the forerunner of despair.' The American astrologer Zolar, by contrast, declares a dream of the Devil to augur 'travel and prosperity', while a British source claims the implication is that the dreamer is hiding a guilty secret. Any encounter with the Devil seems to be generally accepted as a brush with temptation, along with trouble looming in a person's private life. Any child's dream of demons is felt to be a pointer to oncoming illness and a medical check-up is advised. Freudians see an image of a terrifying and lustful father in the Devil, because of the incompatibility between adolescents and fathers.

DIAMONDS

Although dreams of diamonds point to some lucky dealings in business they can equally lead to problems in personal matters. For centuries the diamond has been looked upon as an ageless symbol of beauty, but it has its sinister side, too. To imagine losing some of the precious stones is a sign of ill health; while to buy or sell them will lead to unhappiness. A dream of stealing diamonds will similarly result in financial difficulties. A French source also says that to dream of finding a diamond indicates getting a good lover!

DIGGING
Dreams of digging have long had a special significance in books of rural life, the most widely quoted reference being that the dreamer will always have to work hard. To dig a hole and discover something within is an omen of good news, but if the hole appears to be bottomless or shrouded in mist then watch out for problems. Should the digging uncover a body then this is symbolic of infidelity, according to an American almanac. To see other people digging signifies the dreamer could expect a promotion at work. Recently, a somewhat optimistic British source suggested that this dream could actually be a specific instruction to go searching for buried treasure.

DIRTY CLOTHES
Another very widely reported dream in which sleepers have seen themselves covered with dirt, with varying implications. In the Middle Ages, anyone who dreamed of finding their clothes particularly filthy could wake up happy in the knowledge that it signified they would escape a contagious disease. From about the seventeenth century, European sources noted that people had dreams in which dirt and muck were thrown at them. This was taken as a warning that enemies would try to ruin the subject's reputation. Of late, some authorities have become convinced the dream signifies personal neglect requiring medical attention; while stepping into dirt has curiously been redefined as signifying that a person's affairs are about to prosper.

DISEASES
One of those curious contrary dreams: to imagine having a disease bodes well for the future. Lovers especially can take

this as a sign of happiness and German dream lore says that to imagine suffering from a totally unknown disease is a sign of a big financial gain. Some old English almanacs maintain that anyone who dreams of other people suffering from disease will also come into money — but illegally! The French claim that for a young girl to imagine having an incurable disease means she will have a long and happy life.

DISGUISE
Dreams in which the sleeper sees himself in disguise have only been reported during the last century, and are generally taken as symbolising a subconscious desire on the dreamer's part to obtain a goal by subterfuge. British sources suggest that the dreamer could be seriously embarrassed if he or she carries out the plan. In America, however, the dream is said to be a prediction about making a long trip and probably changing residence; while any dream in which others are disguised heralds some important and beneficial event. The Italians feel that dreams featuring disguise are a warning that someone is trying to trick the dreamer.

DISTANCES
To imagine being a long distance from home, or from the important people in life, is most widely interpreted to mean the dreamer is about to go on a long journey of which he or she has, as yet, no inkling. American dream lore tends to feel it is a warning of disappointments to come, in particular falling under the influence of strangers who will have an adverse effect. Since the Middle Ages, European almanacs have referred to husbands and wives seeing their partners at a distance as symbolising unfaithfulness in the other.

DIVORCE
According to virtually all authorities, a dream of divorce is a sign that the dreamer's marriage is on the firmest

foundation! Conversely, if single people have this dream they should take a long, hard look at their lovers who are probably deceiving them. To dream of relatives or friends being divorced is also, according to British sources, a warning about gossip being spread about you or your partner; while to imagine going through the actual divorce procedure indicates prosperity ahead.

DOCTOR

The doctor is a universal figure of respect and has long been considered as a good omen in any dream. The manner in which the doctor is seen, either professionally or socially, does have a bearing on the dream. In general, to visit a surgery augurs well for future health, while to encounter an MD in the world at large signifies success in endeavours. American almanacs claim that to have a doctor visit you is a sign of wealth; while to call one for children indicates new interests on the way. To dream of being a doctor is also a good omen of happiness and a fulfilled life.

DOG

The dog has been man's best friend throughout history and similarly finds a place in dream lore where the animal is generally acknowledged to be a good omen. Well-behaved white or light-coloured dogs in dreams are a sign of good relations with family and friends. Equally, black dogs can indicate problems with friends, all the more so if they fight and bark. In general, the demeanour of the dog is the clue to what the future holds. Some European authorities maintain that to dream of a small dog points to a frivolous nature; while if the animal is in less than good health, watch out for business problems. Of the definitions which have been given to specific types of dogs, an American almanac lists the two most interesting as: a bulldog, which signifies to a man that he will quarrel with his girlfriend; and a greyhound which warns a female she is about to be seduced. A German listing adds that to see a dog and a bitch mating will lead to the dreamer satisfying all his or her desires!

DOORWAYS
Another very ancient dream symbol, governed by whether the door is open or closed. An open door with a pleasant view beyond it is a pointer to success in the dreamer's plans, while closed doors are said to be symbolic of frustration and missed opportunities. European sources claim that a slamming door is a warning against speculation and gambling, and a door that has to be broken down harbours problems. Several British authorities state that being unable to pass through an open doorway can actually be a sign of long life and happiness; while a house which has a number of doorways is indicating the dreamer has several options in future plans. An old Scandinavian almanac reports that a woman who dreams of entering a doorway in pouring rain is about to enter a life of debauchery.

DRINKING
Although many authorities believe it is the kind of drink that is seen while asleep that is important, a more general interpretation is that the dream of drunkenness is symbolic of dissatisfaction with life. Clear drinks are said to be omens of achievement while cloudy mixtures predict losses. A woman who dreams of 'hilarious drinking', to quote a European almanac, can expect to find herself having an affair; while to partake of a sweet, syrupy drink presages passionate love for either sex. Curiously, according to one American source, to imagine becoming drunk in a dream predicts riches.

DROWNING
The awful sensation of drowning is widely agreed to portend losses, particularly in business. To imagine someone else drowning, especially a partner, is equally ill-omened, unless the dreamer goes to their rescue. In this case he or

she can expect an improvement in status thanks to the help of important friends. American dream lore further maintains that to rescue children from drowning is a promise of prosperity.

DUCKS

Rural almanacs from as far back as the fourteenth century refer to ducks seen in dreams as being birds of good omen, especially when viewed flying overhead. For young girls this is a sign of a happy marriage and children, while for men success at work. On water, ducks predict some good news on the way, while the dreamer who imagines shooting a duck had better be careful the next time he or she travels, as the risk of an accident is high. Both British and American books of dream lore speak of eating duck as a foretaste of fame and fortune.

E

EAGLE

The Eagle is regarded in dream lore as the 'king of the aerial universe' and accorded the same respect as the lion. In ancient Egypt he was seen as the symbol of royalty and divinity, and has subsequently become the sign of imperial conquest for several nations including the Romans, and Napoleon's France. Today, the eagle flies high as the national symbol of the United States of America. The bird, therefore, equates in dreams to a desire for conquest, power and domination. An eagle in flight is a good omen for business, while one perching on a mountain top foretells the realisation of ambitions. To be attacked by an eagle, however, indicates problems, and to see one injured signifies problems in love. For several hundred years, books of dream lore have also claimed that the pregnant woman who dreams of an eagle will give birth to a famous son.

EARS

The ancient Egyptians were first to record dreams in which human ears featured, and concluded they signified the dreamer would soon hear some exciting news. In the homes of the wealthy in medieval Europe, dreams of people having the ears of a donkey were interpreted as meaning that the household servants could be trusted; while the ears of a dog were said to show trust between a

husband and wife! Any kind of problem with the ears —
such as a loss of hearing, injury or deformity — is said to be
ill-omened, probably presaging trouble from an unexpected source. The French believe that any dream of
attractive ears signifies a love-affair.

EARTH
The earth has always been given a maternal meaning in
dream lore, for not only does it provide so much that
humanity needs to sustain itself, but it is also a final resting
place. The Chinese believed that to dream of earth covered
by flourishing crops indicated luck and prosperity, while
throughout Europe the sight of ploughed earth foretold a
happy domestic life and devoted children. Several British
sources have also stated that to dream of being buried in
earth is a sign of financial benefit. Earthquakes have also
been a feature of dreams since the days of antiquity when
they were believed to foretell turmoil or war. Today any
such experience points to problems ahead, which may well
call for a change of environment. An interesting recent
survey from America revealed that a number of people
beginning analysis or therapeutic treatment have reported
having dreams of earthquakes.

EATING
Another very ancient dream, in which a vision of sharing a
meal with members of the family is said to indicate happy
times ahead. In earlier centuries, a dream of a group of
strangers eating was believed to herald the downfall of an
enemy. The person who dreams of eating alone should
be prepared for a period of depression, while to overeat
(according to Russian lore) presages the discovery of some
valuable items! If the meal consists of specific items of
food then consult the appropriate sections in this book.
Any repast which is brought to a sudden halt by the food
being removed is a sign of problems with members of the

dreamer's family, or those at work who are dependent on him or her.

EAVESDROPPING
Overhearing the conversation of others has proved to be a much more widely recorded dream than might be expected, though the words spoken are usually described as unintelligible. According to the consensus of opinion, the dream signifies good fortune, usually in the form of some financial benefits. European almanacs think the luck will manifest itself in the form of success with the opposite sex. If the dreamer imagines being overheard in this way, says a British book of dream lore, then it is a warning he or she is facing a dilemma which will be difficult to resolve.

ECSTASY
Authorities are divided on the significance of any dream in which the sleeper experiences ecstasy and a general feeling of abandonment. Several nineteenth-century books of dream lore are discreetly insistent the sensation of ecstasy points to a visit from a long-absent friend. More recent European sources believe it signifies that the dreamer is experiencing a sense of boredom with his or her sex life, and should do something about enlivening it.

EGGS
Eggs are symbolic of good news, except if the dreamer drops or breaks them in which case watch out for quarrels or money losses. From about the fourteenth century, to dream of finding a nest of hen's eggs was said to denote wealth for men and many happy love-affairs for women. White and brown eggs are variously said to be harbingers of good and bad news. To imagine eating eggs is a pointer to good health, though if the eggs are bad then watch out for problems among family or friends. According to an American almanac, for a woman to dream of cooking eggs foretells she is going to become the subject of a lot of wicked

gossip among her friends. And an amusing Victorian book of omens adds that anyone who dreams of being spattered by eggs is actually going to come into money — though it will be 'of doubtful origin'!

ELECTION
To participate in some form of election is a dream of comparatively recent date, and though now generally regarded as a good omen, Victorian almanacs believed it foretold becoming engaged in a controversy that would adversely affect a person's social or financial standing. European and British sources are now agreed that the omens point to success in any current plans. Though one turn-of-the-century American almanac claimed that to imagine winning an election should put the dreamer on guard against the ideas of a treacherous friend!

ELEPHANT
In the East, the elephant has for centuries been held as a sign of good fortune and the growth of wisdom. In India, it is believed that for a poor person to dream of elephants points to a more prosperous future, and that to imagine riding one, predicts social esteem. Elephants at work are a sign of business success, and to see them drinking, say the Indians, means the dreamer will receive help from an influential person. An American source maintains that dreams of elephants in captivity are ill-omened, presaging family quarrels; while to see one in a circus could mean the death of a member of the family.

ELOPING
The dream of running off with a member of the opposite sex exercised the minds of many almanac writers in the eighteenth and nineteenth centuries, who were, no doubt, gratified to find it proved a case of contrary. To dream of eloping actually presages a problem in a person's love-life: if the

dreamer is single it is a sign his or her partner is being unfaithful, while if married it warns of imminent exposure. If a dreamer imagines his partner eloping this is also a sign of unfaithfulness. In some sources, though, this dream has been labelled as a flight from reality requiring the dreamer to face up to their besetting problems.

EMBARRASSED
Quite simply, the more embarrassed the dreamer felt the better the omens for future success and well-being. This is accepted as one of the best examples of a contrary dream, and many books of dream lore have claimed that any lover experiencing embarrassment can be assured of a happy courtship. Even a dream in which other people are embarrassed is a sign of happiness, though some authorities also urge the dreamer to take it as a warning, and rely on personal judgement rather than the advice of others.

EMIGRATING
A particularly European-orientated dream which has been variously defined during the past two centuries. On the one hand, it is seen as symbolic of a deep unhappiness requiring change; on the other, presaging a letter from a friend in a foreign country. In several Iron Curtain countries dreams in which trouble with emigration authorities occur are said to indicate great happiness ahead. An early twentieth-century American book of dream lore records that a dream of being refused admission to a country by immigration authorities indicates danger because of some hidden secret. In its most general terms, the dream foretells unexpected demands on resources which will require careful economies.

ENEMY
The old soothsayers used to give comfort and encouragement to kings and noblemen who had experienced vivid

dreams about their enemies by telling them the omens were auspicious — they could now rely on good fortune to attend them. In recent times, dream lore has claimed that the more a dreamer is attacked and defamed by an enemy, the greater will be his success at work; and to outsmart an enemy is a sign of winning a legal dispute. To dream of someone specific, who is suspected of being an enemy, is a clear indication of having loyal friends who can be relied upon.

ENGINES
Engines, regardless of type, have always been seen in dreams as symbolic of problems — especially where any future travelling plans are concerned. The Victorians believed that to imagine a broken-down engine presaged misfortune, and that any of the dreamer's objectives in life would be seriously delayed. To dream of actually working on an engine points to an imminent and enforced change in work and/or home. By contrast, to see an engineer in a dream, predicts great happiness, according to a recent study of dreams.

ENVELOPE
Another object increasingly noted in modern dreams, especially those envelopes that are sealed or cannot be opened. For many years the envelope itself has been regarded as an omen of unhappy news. A sealed envelope can be indicative of problems looming in the future, or alternatively a sign that others are keeping secrets from the dreamer which will necessitate him or her being less trusting. An open envelope is also a worrying sign, though the problems can be overcome by determination. American almanacs state that to dream of posting a letter foretells good luck, though to receive an envelope, which on being opened proves to contain several letters, is a warning of a big disappointment in love.

ESCAPE

Dreams of escape from accidents, confinement or difficulties are almost as old as mankind and invariably favourable. To avoid injury ensures a happy life; to escape from any form of prison, a rapid rise in business; and to avoid difficulties, success in personal affairs. Numerous books of dream lore have put great store on escaping from fire or water dangers, though to escape from attack, particularly by an animal, is a warning about plans to slander and defraud the dreamer. A recent British almanac assures its readers that these dreams are merely symbolic of a lack of self confidence. A similar American publication says that any dream in which relatives or friends are unable to escape from danger promises them financial gain!

EVIL

A dream of evil is not a nightmare but an experience in which the atmosphere is bad and peopled by evil spirits. It is a warning of troubles ahead, particularly in business. Some sources urge a major rethink of objectives after such a dream, particularly if the spirits took on specific forms that in any way resembled business rivals. A medical examination might also be advisable.

EXAMINATION

With examinations playing such a vital role in most people's lives, it is hardly surprising to discover that dreams of these mental trials are frequently recorded and have come in for considerable study. Dreaming of taking an examination before the event occurs is now seen as symbolic of a need for further study. Both European and American sources are also agreed that to dream of failing an examination, or being unable to answer questions, is a warning the dreamer may have set unreasonably high objectives; while to pass in comfort is a sign that success in life will be enjoyed as a whole. In Britain, a dream of children passing their exams can be very comforting to parents, for it presages that their ambitions for their off-spring will be realised. Modern authorities are agreed that examination dreams symbolise a feeling of being put to the test on some important issue in life, which the dreamer is afraid they will not pass.

EXCHANGE

The act of exchanging is generally thought to be inauspicious in dreams, though an American source says to change an item in a store will lead to the recovery of lost valuables! The consensus of opinion is that this dream foreshadows business problems, though if the items were being exchanged with family members, a period of unhappiness will follow in the home. A Victorian almanac amusingly reports that a young woman who dreams of exchanging her sweetheart with a friend would probably do well to follow this course of action as she would be happier with another man!

EXCREMENT

Since antiquity, excrement has been seen as symbolising wealth: the famous Assyrian *Book of Dreams* reported that to imagine eating faeces foretells coming into a fortune; while Artemidorus declared that 'to be smeared with excrement is an excellent prediction for poor people'. Roman sources also believed that to dream of having a bowel movement would deliver a person from their worries; hence the argument of some modern authorities that the experience is also associated with a liberation of inhibitions or repressions. In Europe, in the Middle Ages, to dream of stepping on excrement foretold acquiring money (as it still does today), though to imagine being constipated was a warning against avarice and stubborness. Modern sources agree that the more embarrassing the situation the better the omen — in particular, to dream of having a bowel movement in bed (an inheritance), or in a public place (financial success in business).

EXERCISE

Dreams of taking vigorous exercise are not just phenomena of the modern health-conscious age. Books of dream lore which appeared more than 300 years ago also listed the omens. Strenuous physical activity is considered a sign of well-being, particularly if it is undertaken with a partner or members of the family. If the activity exhausts the dreamer before waking, then this is also a happy indication of lots of social activities in the future — according to most almanacs. In America, the tired dreamer is warned to be careful about monetary losses; but, if others in the dream seem more exhausted, then some difficult problem is about to be solved.

EXPLORING

Most authorities are agreed that to dream of going on an expedition of any kind is a fairly straightforward sign of making an essential journey in the near future. However, to fail in any kind of exploration points to problems at work, and to imagine others as explorers indicates that arguments with family are brewing. To meet any well-known explorer has been curiously defined as meaning the dreamer has several untrustworthy friends.

EXPLOSIONS

For centuries, to dream of explosives or explosions was believed to indicate arguments in either business or family life. According to a seventeenth-century almanac, a dream of an explosion portended a scandal, and the dreamer could expect a lot of antagonism in social circles if he or she was blackened by the explosion or saw the atmosphere filled with smoke. A hundred years later, a book of romantic dream lore for young ladies warned them that if they saw flames or were enveloped by an explosion, they were in imminent danger of seduction. Today, the dream is more generally interpreted as being a warning against trying to settle arguments by emotional reactions.

EYES

Many omens have been attributed to eyes in dream lore — specifying colour, shape, size, and so on — though few dreams on record are that specific. A general sensation of being looked at by many eyes is felt to be a subconscious questioning of the dreamer's motivations in recent activities; while to see smiling, beautiful eyes predicts love and happiness. Any kind of injury to eyes is a warning to take care in future business dealings; and to see crossed eyes presages financial success. A Spanish almanac adds that to dream of a single eye, or a one-eyed person, is an omen of losing a partner to a rival in love.

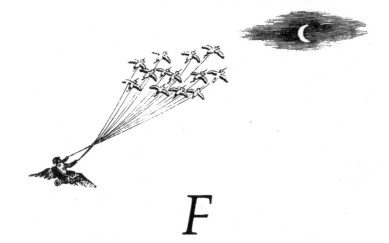

F

FACE

One of the oldest of all dreams and found recorded in the lore of the ancient civilisations of Egypt and Rome. The earliest writers believed the face was invariably that of a departed friend or relative who invaded the dreamer's sleep with a message. If the face did not speak, its aspect was the clue to the message — a smiling visage portending good luck, and one creased with worry or anger pointing to unhappiness and death. According to European dream books, if a young man or woman glimpsed a loved one's face much-aged, it meant an end to the affair, while a married person who saw his or her own face was being warned of divorce. A recent American almanac says that a dreamer plagued by faces he or she cannot identify is about to move house.

FACTORY

The Victorians were fascinated by dreams in which work featured, in particular those about busy factories, as these were said to be good omens that if the dreamer worked hard he or she was bound to succeed. Nineteenth-century almanacs also noted that a dream of entering a factory or seeing oneself at work in such a place was a sign of beneficial changes on the way. A curious German book of about 1900 even lists the best factories to imagine working in:

metal and clothing factories feature at the top as being symbolic of long life!

FAILURE
Another of those strange dreams which is quite the opposite of what it seems: the worse the failure, the better the achievement the dreamer will enjoy. Dream books, since the days of the colourful monarch Charles II, have encouraged lovers who dream of failing to win their heart's desire to persevere in real life as success is guaranteed. The businessman who fails in a dream has only to apply himself with renewed energy to fulfil all his ambitions. Only a dream of relatives failing in some project is deemed to be a cautionary note to a dreamer's business dealings, according to recent American sources.

FALLING
Dreams of falling are among the most common throughout the world, and symbolic of a basic mental struggle going on in the dreamer's life. The fear can range from business failure to sexual inadequacy, and curiously the longer the fall, in the dream, the sooner the problem is likely to be resolved. The oldest almanacs stated that to fall from a high mountain symbolised misfortune — unless the dreamer was unhurt at the end of the fall, in which case the setback would be only temporary. However, to fall and be hurt pointed to real hardships and loss of friends. Some European sources say that to fall into water, of any kind, is a death omen; while an American almanac cites falling from a bridge as a warning of impending madness! According to this same manual, to dream of other people falling is a happier sign, suggesting promotion at work.

FAME
To dream of being famous — and who hasn't done so in everyday life? — is not an uncommon sensation in sleep, though the omens are far from auspicious. Victorian

almanacs upbraided readers who dreamed of becoming famous, with the message that this presaged 'disappointed aspirations' — although to dream about famous people 'portends your rise from obscurity to a place of honour'! Today, authorities suggest these dreams are actually an indication that a person is striving after something which is really out of reach, and that his or her sights should be lowered. One American source claims that a wife who dreams of her husband becoming famous is actually in for a nasty shock — it means he is now in love with another woman!

FAMILY
For anyone to dream about their family is a good omen and points to a happy time for all the members, as well as excellent health. Naturally enough, the reverse is true if any members of the family appear ill or argumentative. According to a recent British almanac, dreaming of a family reunion is perhaps the most satisfying dream of all, as it signifies the dreamer is better loved than he or she might believe.

FARM
Without exception, British rural almanacs describe any dream of living on a well-stocked and cared-for farm as a fortunate omen, though they make no bones of the fact that the life can be hard and tiring. If the farm is in a poor state then expect to lose some money. In Europe, to visit a farm denotes making some new and pleasant friends, while in Australia a dream of buying a farm signifies a profitable deal for the businessman. Curiously, in America, where these omens also hold true, it is said that to dream of a farm on fire, foretells considerable wealth! According to a recent British study, the farmer who features in a dream is a compensatory figure who recalls the world of nature, from which contemporary humanity has lost contact.

69

FASHION

To imagine oneself in or out of fashion is a dream only noted in recent years and defined as being symbolic of a deep-rooted need for smart clothes, and being seen in the right places. A French dream dictionary says dreams of attending a fashion show, or of seeing models parading, signifies a long life. An American source claims that to imagine looking at fashion models in a department store window presages quarrels among members of the dreamer's family.

FATHER

Dreams about a father, whether he is still alive or dead, have long been thought to foretell problems, for which the dreamer will require good advice in order to solve them. A number of British sources on dream lore state that if the father is dead, the dream presages business worries for a man. But for a girl to dream of her late father is a warning that her lover is being unfaithful. In Europe a dream of a male parent dying while his is still alive also foretells problems at work. Several American sources state that a scolding father — or mother — in a dream denotes arguments and stress.

FEAR

To experience fear during a dream is not as worrying as it might seem at the time. In fact, several authorities are convinced the dream predicts that the sleeper will be able to face up to his or her problems and overcome them. The Victorian almanacs claimed that to feel fear, from any source, was an indication that future engagements would not prove as successful as expected, while young ladies should beware of an unhappy love-affair. To dream persistently of being afraid is, according to an American book of dream lore, a sign the dreamer is a person of great courage.

FEEDING

Dreams of personally feeding children, the hungry, and even animals have been noted since biblical times and are universally accepted as omens of good fortune and prosperity. Only if the dreamer sees someone else doing the feeding should he or she be cautious, for European sources claim this is a sign that the sleeper is being deceived.

FEET

The Victorians believed that to dream of one's own feet was an omen of despair, but modern authorities have summarised the whole range of dreams about feet as a warning, to the people involved, to watch where their bad habits might be taking them! During the Middle Ages a dream of naked feet signified intimacy with the opposite sex, and feet being washed indicated a release from anxiety. Dreams in which feet are hurt point to troubles of a humiliating nature, though for at least two centuries, visions of painful bunions have been said to foretell a comfortable old age! Two omens about feet are believed to be just as valid, asleep or awake: itchy feet forecast travel, while cold feet mean a disappointment in love.

FERRY

A journey across a river by a ferryboat continues to be a widely recorded dream. The significant aspects being the width of the river, and the time taken to cross. The longer the voyage the better the dreamer's prospects of success in life; as long as the water was calm and clear, and the ferry reached the other side *before* the dream ended. American almanacs report that to see lots of other people on board is a sign of success in love.

FIGHTING

Dreams of being involved in a fight have exercised the minds of almanac writers for several centuries, different meanings being attributed to the various kinds of fighting:

a spontaneous scrap, a bout of boxing, or any form of combat with weapons. In essence, the dream is symbolic of the dreamer's combative spirit, though it should be read in conjunction with what is an obvious need for change. A century ago, for a man to dream of seeing others fighting was an omen he was squandering time and money; while for a woman to see her man fighting indicated he was unworthy. A recent American book of dream lore says that to be beaten in a fight presages opposition in love-affairs.

FINGERS
The Romans were the first to believe that to dream of beautiful hands was a good omen for loving and being loved. Hands that were bloodied or injured in some way presaged trouble and suffering, while actually to lose fingers indicated a loss of money. Pointing fingers are recorded in dreams from the fifteenth century, and foretell a change of residence. Long fingers are a sign of a short marriage, say a number of European sources, and short fingers indicate an inheritance is on the way. In Australia, any dream which features a hand with fewer than five fingers is said to signify joy and love.

FIRE
The ancient oracles considered fire symbolic of formidable power which could only be mastered with difficulty, and they associated it with love, passion and sexuality. The key to dreams about fire, though, is whether the dreamer has the impression of being burned. To merely see a fire is an omen of good news, but to be scorched by one presages trouble. For several centuries, European almanacs have claimed that to witness a building on fire is a good sign, even if it is one closely associated with the dreamer's life. A burning home, for example, points to a happy domestic life, while an office or shop ablaze signifies a rush of business. A number of books of dream lore also state that to imagine poking a fire is a sign of a new love-affair, but a fire

raging out of control is a warning to control your temper. An American source adds that to start a fire indicates the dreamer is about to be seduced!

FISH
The ancient Babylonians dreamed many fantasies about fish and equated its shape with that of a phallic symbol. Since the establishment of the Christian era, however, when the fish was embraced as a religious emblem, the creature has been regarded as a dream omen of good fortune when seen swimming about in clear water — probably foretelling travel. To dream of catching a fish indicates that the sleeper will be loved by family and friends. Dead fish are omens of disillusionment and disappointment in business, according to later European sources; while in Britain to dream of eating fish is a sign that current ambitions will be successful. In general terms, the fish symbolises a healthy, cheerful state of mind.

FLAGS
Since the Middle Ages, most European and eastern nations have believed that dreams of their national flags presaged good fortune and prosperity. While the flags of enemy nations are obviously ill-omened, plain white flags indicate success in personal ventures, and red banners warn against arguments and quarrels. A number of Victorian books of dream lore prophesied that for a young woman to dream of a flag meant she would be seduced by a soldier. More recently, flags have been seen as symbolic of travel, though to dream of carrying or raising one in the air is a pointer to improvements in wealth and standard of living.

FLEET
Maritime almanacs have for centuries declared that to dream of a naval fleet at sea is an omen of a letter from a loved one, though not necessarily someone who is at sea. A curious eighteenth-century German source maintains that

73

to see a large fleet under way presages some dramatic changes in business, though a more recent American publication ascribes a quite different interpretation: the dreamer is being deceived by his or her lover! Among all seafaring nations, dreams of fishing fleets are said to be good omens, though care in family relationships is advised when the fishermen are seen trawling in bad weather.

FLIES
Surprisingly common in dreams, these universally disliked insects are today believed to symbolise ill-health, and a medical check-up is advised. For centuries, flies have been seen as omens of sickness and contagion, as well as a possible warning concerning enemies who are about to surround the dreamer. In America, a swarm of flies is believed to signify petty annoyances which are about to arise. The French maintain that a woman who dreams of flies faces a period of unhappiness. To kill the flies during the course of the dream will happily mitigate most of the consequences, says a British source.

FLOODS
Authorities are at odds about the significance of a dream in which floods occur. Certainly, until the last century, most books of dream lore thought they presaged ill-health and unhappiness, though nowadays several writers have insisted the dreamer will enjoy good fortune later in life. In America, a dream of flooding is said to indicate that a person's worries are about to be smoothed away, while in Europe it means that a few problems lie ahead, although nothing that cannot be overcome by determination. A French almanac adds that for a dreamer to be swept away by floods is a sign that he or she is being deceived by a lover.

FLOWERS
A dream of flowers in bloom has always been seen as an omen of sincerity, affection and passion. Even flowers

which may be wilting or have passed their best are merely a warning against over-confidence. For many centuries, young girls who dreamed of receiving a bouquet of flowers could soon expect a suitor to come calling, while gathering wild flowers was said to signify an exciting adventure with a member of the opposite sex. In short, flowers are a most pleasant subject to dream about!

FLYING
Dreams of flying are widely and frequently recorded, and though Freud has declared their significance to be purely sexual (a desire for greater prowess), other authorities believe them to symbolise a yearning for liberty and transcendence. The Babylonians maintained the dreamer was being warned about instability in his life, while the Romans saw it as an assurance that the dreamer would rise above other, more common, men and women. In essence, though, the dream represents the sleeper's basic ambition, and if the flight took them steadily on a medium level course they can expect to attain their objectives without too much difficulty. A wearying flight striving constantly upwards is, conversely, a warning that the dreamer has probably set his goals too high and they need readjustment. Some modern authorities believe the dream can also follow a particular achievement that has left the sleeper feeling 'high' on excitement and stimulation.

FOG
To imagine being lost in a dense fog is surely one of the eeriest dreams, though these night visions have only been on record for the past two centuries. For men, this is a sign of business worries; while for a woman a warning of some impending scandal in which she may become involved, unless she is careful about those with whom she associates. A recent British source claims the dream indicates that something is slowing the dreamer down in life, though all the authorities are agreed that to emerge from the fog,

before waking, promises a successful outcome to the problems.

FOOD
Roman sources first declared that dreams of food indicated monetary gain and sensual pleasures, though any food that looked or seemed to taste bad was a warning of humiliation and dishonour. In China, to imagine having the face or hands smeared with food was a sign of poverty, though to dream of buying it would result in a big family celebration. European authorities in the seventeenth century, claimed that to dream of not having enough food was an instance of contrary and would lead to the downfall of an enemy. Modern sources are agreed that food is symbolic of stability, and to waste or spoil meals is a sign of domestic problems to come.

FOOTBALL
Another dream of comparatively recent origin, particularly noted in Britain and Europe, and about which the omens are mixed. To be a spectator at a game is generally accepted to be a warning against becoming negative about your life and equally to be careful about making new friends. Conversely, to dream of playing football promises success in business ventures, and to score a goal presages a financial windfall. Strangely, a German book of dream lore maintains that to miss an open goal in a dream game indicates a long life!

FORD
The ford, or shallow water crossing, is a common dream image which has been noted since antiquity and is said to symbolise change. The dream invariably arises at decisive moments in life, when the dreamer is being faced with a choice of going in one direction or another. But authorities are agreed that the deeper meaning will only be established by remembering what stood on the banks on either side of

the ford, the means by which it was crossed, and whether the water was deep or shallow.

FOREST

Forests have featured in dream lore since the Middle Ages and are generally perceived as good omens. Several European almanacs state that to be alone in a forest bodes well for the dreamer's social life, although to feel afraid indicates being let down by someone close. American sources claim that if the trees are tall and stately, then business success lies ahead, but to imagine hiding in a forest suggests the dreamer is avoiding facing up to some problems. Perversely, all authorities are agreed that to dream of a forest on fire symbolises impending good news.

FORTUNE-TELLING

A popular dream according to several almanacs, though with diametrically opposed omens. If the dreamer is having his or her fortune told then there are problems ahead whatever the dream-reading may indicate; while to be the fortune-teller presages good news, especially in business dealings. Victorian books of dream lore claimed that young ladies who had visions of having their fortunes told would soon be faced with making a choice between two suitors competing for their love. In Europe, to dream of someone else having their fortune told is said to indicate a close friend whose advice can be sought and relied upon to solve any pressing problem.

FOX

The fox is a vivid dream image and for centuries the omens of seeing one have been clear: it is a symbol of danger in the form of an enemy or rival who should be watched carefully. More recently, the creature has been said to signify that someone is trying to trick the dreamer, and only by honesty will these plans be thwarted. Some European almanacs state that to dream of chasing a fox denotes the person is engaging in a doubtful business venture or a risky love-affair. To see a fox killed is widely accepted to presage success in all undertakings.

FRECKLES
All romantic dream books consider freckles to be an omen of popularity with the opposite sex, though at least one eighteenth-century almanac claims that a woman who dreams of having a freckled face is going to suffer a number of displeasing incidents in the near future. Several European sources believe that to dream of someone else being covered with freckles indicates that a love-affair is about to develop; while for the dreamer to see his or her own face covered with freckles in a mirror presages the loss of a lover.

FRIENDS
One of the most straightforward of dreams: if the friends are cheerful and in good health then pleasing news and happy times are forthcoming. But the authorities agree that if the friends in the dream are sick or troubled, then the omens are bad — foretelling illness in the dreamer's own family. Most sources also state that to dream of a friend who is abroad, or has not been heard from for some time, presages the arrival of news about them relevant to the circumstances in which they are seen.

FROGS
Frogs are today considered in dream lore as omens of good luck, symbolising success in business and in love-affairs. Some Victorian almanacs, however, felt that to dream about them in marshy places foretold mounting problems, while to actually catch one denoted carelessness in matters of health. In contrast, modern authorities believe they signify good friends, and in concert with that fact, personal contentment. In America, a woman who sees a bullfrog can expect to marry a wealthy man, and to see the creatures

swimming in water presages a gift of money. Perhaps not surprisingly, the French claim that to dream of eating frogs also signifies the dreamer will become wealthy!

FUNERAL

This is one more of those strange dreams where the omens are in complete contrast to the implications. The authorities are unanimous: to witness a funeral presages good news. In Britain, for example, the dream symbolises a wedding or an engagement, though the Americans say it indicates luck in love. Throughout Europe, to imagine being present at your own funeral is a sign of the end of some persistent problems; while in the Far East, long life and happiness is being prophesied. Only the Scandinavians, apparently, believe that to dream of being a pall bearer at a funeral is a warning against making a hasty or foolish decision.

FUTURE

A popular nineteenth-century volume of dream lore states, rather amusingly, under this heading: 'To dream of the future is a prognostic of careful reckoning and avoidance of detrimental extravagance'. Today's views seem to vary regarding the omens of a dream where the subject finds him or herself in a future scenario. The European opinion is that the vision symbolises a sudden and unexpected change in life, though in America the contention is that it presents the dreamer with a chance to resolve an old quarrel. In Russia, the omen of a dream of being troubled and impoverished in the future, promises much happiness to come!

G

GAGGED

The sensation of being gagged has recently been the subject of research in Britain and America where it is listed as an obstacle dream. The consensus of opinion is that the dream symbolises difficult problems ahead, though a few authorities have argued it specifically points to the dreamer making — or about to make — an unhappy marriage. A recent Italian book for lovers suggested that for a man to dream of having a gag in his mouth presaged being kissed by a beautiful woman; while a woman could shortly expect to fall in love. To dream of gagging someone else, adds a British source, is a warning about becoming the subject of gossip through some sexual indiscretion.

GALLERY

Dreaming of art galleries has been increasingly recorded in recent years, with the omens mostly being taken as good. Whether the gallery features paintings or sculptures, then financial gains or even a form of civil honour can be expected. If, however, the pictures were specifically old masters, a former friend is going to be welcomed back into the dreamer's life, while if they were the work of modern artists then a significant new friendship is about to be made.

GALLOWS

For several centuries, dreams of the gallows featured prominently in almanacs where they were confidently described as good luck omens! Despite the evil repute of the gallows dotted across Britain, Europe and many other countries of the world, dream lore insisted that the person who dreamed of dying on the scaffold would actually rise to a position of importance in life, and perhaps even inherit a fortune. A cautionary early nineteenth-century British almanac declared that to dream of someone else on the gallows foretold difficult times ahead, and that any young girl who imagined her lover being hung should beware of marrying a cruel and unscrupulous man. Of late, with the abolition of capital punishment in many lands, the dream has been much less recorded. However, instances featuring the electric chair, noted in America, have been similarly ascribed with favourable omens.

GAMBLING

Though many different dreams of gambling have been listed over the years, most authorities believe this to be an instance where the opposite applies. To win heavily is a warning of gambling more than a person can afford to lose; while to suffer a reverse points to some profitable opportunities arising in the near future. American sources claim any gambling dream presages happy social events, while a German authority says that to lose a bet will relieve the dreamer of any pain or ill-health he may be suffering. A recent British work urges a rethink of finances to anyone who has this dream.

GAMES

The Victorian dream books were the first to list omens for games, generally agreeing that they presaged financial gains. Enjoying the game was important for this prophecy to be fulfilled, for any show of bad sportsmanship was said to rebound on the dreamer. Today, most sources view this as a dream of contrary: to win a game indicates trouble on the way; while to lose points to some important and beneficial news. The Americans are more specific, stating that to win a game will lead to loneliness for the dreamer. They also suggest that a dream of children wearing blindfolds and playing games, is a sign the dreamer is being deceived by a member of the opposite sex.

GARDENS

The ancients and the Arabs believed that for a man to dream of a garden symbolised a woman's sexual parts, and to imagine eating fruits in one would lead to wealth and an advantageous marriage. But though Eastern sources in general tended to regard the garden as a special place for lovemaking, in the West it was seen more as a symbol of persevering activity and growth, where human and natural forces met in harmony. Hence seventeenth-century European sources reported that dreams of gardens full of healthy-looking plants and flowers represented great opportunities for love, happiness and material gain. A neglected or barren garden, however, pointed to a loss of love and peace of mind. Victorian almanacs told young girls that a dream of a garden full of vegetables was a sign they would make a happy marriage, while a man who saw a garden of pretty flowers should pursue the object of his affection with greater fervour!

GATE

There are numerous omens on record about gates, several of which contradict each other. In Britain, for instance, dreaming of an open gate signifies opportunities ahead, while in America to pass through the gate means bad news is imminent. The Europeans believe a closed gate is symbolic of insurmountable problems, while in the East a locked gate indicates great business success. What appears to be generally agreed is that the gate symbolises a need for decision and the determination to carry out any such resolutions in order to reach a happy solution.

GEESE
Another bird often recorded in dreams and generally considered to be a good omen. To see geese on water is a sign of improved finances, but if they are flying most European authorities believe this presages a long, but pleasant journey. According to the Canadians, to hear geese quacking indicates a death in the family, though several American sources maintain that dreams of eating geese are a sign of good fortune. In Britain, to dream of a goose being plucked has for hundreds of years been seen as symbolic of gaining an inheritance.

GHOSTS
The ancient Greeks first recorded ghosts in dreams, and, like every generation since, considered them omens of good fortune. Some early writers also believed these apparitions were proof of life after death, and the most comforting of dreams were those in which a relative, such as a mother or father, appeared. In the Middle Ages, dreams in which a ghost spoke were believed to be a warning against any doubtful scheme that was being considered. More recently, this has come to be seen as indicating a breakdown in health which can be avoided by getting medical advice. In several European countries, a dream of a female ghost is believed to indicate wealth.

GIANT
Earlier generations believed that any dream in which a giant appeared presaged success after struggling against the odds — the bigger the giant the better the ultimate rewards would be. In Europe, to be confronted by a giant was seen as a warning to be on guard against the machinations of enemies, and the Spanish believed that to dream of more than one giant pointed to success in love-affairs.

Modern dream lore, however, maintains that the symbolism behind the appearance of any larger-than-life person in a dream is a need for the dreamer to develop more self-confidence.

GIFTS

To dream of receiving a gift is a good omen, especially at the time of a new love-affair where the dreamer's affections will be reciprocated. The first Elizabethans placed great store on such dreams, especially when the gift was made by a relative or friend. In Europe, though, to dream of giving a gift to someone else presages bad luck, in particular falling out with a close friend. American sources have also maintained that to dream of posting a gift is an omen of causing displeasure to others.

GIRL

For a man to dream of a girl is an omen of good fortune and tranquillity — according to most authorities — the only exception being if the girl is seen sitting in a window. This symbolises a forthcoming dispute with a member of the opposite sex. Should the girl be a beautiful stranger, then the lucky dreamer can look forward to some unexpected and happy news. To imagine kissing 'the girl of your dreams' presages success in both business and personal life. Dreams in which men imagine themselves to be girls have also been listed by several almanacs — one Victorian book declaring rather ridiculously that the dreamer will be 'weak-minded, or become an actor and play female parts'. More recently, this dream has been declared symptomatic of a sexual problem for which advice should be sought.

GLASS

Glass has featured extensively in American dream lore where any piece is seen as a symbol of good luck and prosperity. To look through a window-pane symbolises a prosperous future, though if the dreamer has to polish the glass beware of complacency in business matters. Naturally enough to dream of breaking glass — in particular a mirror — indicates problems ahead, possibly even a death in the family. In Europe, dirty glassware is symbolic of domestic unhappiness, while in the East any dream of glassware points to a birth. In Britain, to cut a piece of glass is said to be an indication that the dreamer may have upset someone more than they realise and should try to make amends.

GLOVES
Almanac writers in the seventeenth century first paid special attention to gloves in dreams, believing that smart and stylish gloves pointed to a happy and stable future, while old and ragged ones were a sure sign of betrayal and loss. To lose a pair of gloves presaged being deserted by someone close, and to imagine pulling them off indicated problems in business. In the twentieth century, however, old gloves have become symbolic of happiness, though getting them dirty is said to be indicative of trouble and loneliness. The most popular definition in books of dream lore claims that to find a pair of gloves during a dream will lead to a new love-affair.

GOD
Over the years, Christian almanacs have devoted many pages to dreams concerning God, declaring them to presage much happiness and contentment. Authorities on dream lore, however, consider them to be particularly rare dreams, and ones which require honest self-appraisal and humility for the omens to be fulfilled. Curiously, a late eighteenth-century American book of dream lore declared that any dream of worshipping God was a pointer to sickness in the family. A British volume of the same period came up with an even more astonishing definition, seemingly aimed at male readers: 'If you dream of seeing God,' the book declared, 'you will be domineered over by a

tyrannical woman masquerading under the cloak of Christianity.'

GOLD
To see anything gold in a dream has been generally accepted for centuries to indicate success in current enterprises, while to actually find some of this precious metal symbolises increased financial rewards. The earliest writers on dream lore believed that gold symbolised honour and recognition, though it was the Romans who declared that to dream of stealing gold was a warning that the dreamer was being tempted into dishonesty. Today's authorities believe the dream is also a caution against placing too much reliance on monetary matters, to the detriment of personal relationships and health.

GOLF
A dream much more frequently recorded among men than woman and, in general terms, believed to presage good luck, especially if the dreamer is playing well. A Victorian almanac declares that the more holes a dreamer wins, the more his wishes will be fulfilled; while a Canadian book published 50 years ago, claims the dream signifies the golfer's wife will soon give birth! An American source says that a bad score warns the dreamer to be on his guard against the advice of untrustworthy friends; while a British publication maintains that if a dispute breaks out during the game, the dreamer is shortly going to be humiliated by someone. Recent study has also suggested that a dream of golf may well point to dealings with the opposite sex — the success, or otherwise of the match, indicating the dreamer's prospects.

GOSSIP
A popular topic with almanac writers since the Middle Ages, virtually all of whom have declared this to be a dream of contrary. The worse the gossip the dreamer imagines

being talked about himself, the better the omens and the happier the news to be received. Should the dreamer gossip about others, then this also is a pointer to realising some long-standing ambitions, say these same sources. Recently, though, some new authorities have cautioned that a dream of gossip could equally be a warning of possible embarrassment caused by careless talk.

GOVERNMENT .
There are some interesting dreams on record by people who imagined themselves in high governmental positions — and they were not all politicians, or men and women with ambitions to rule! Since the late 1800s, dreams of being involved in government have been explained by American sources as omens of a forthcoming series of happy social engagements. In Europe, however, the signs are reversed and the dreamer can expect a period of uncertainty. In France, to dream of being offered a government post is said to presage domestic upheavals.

GRANDPARENTS
Another dream noted since the days of antiquity, and one tempered with a mixture of omens. For a dreamer to see his or her grandparents and talk to them, is a sign of forthcoming difficulties which can, nonetheless, be overcome by acting sensibly and listening to good advice. According to several European authorities, the grandparents are seen as symbolising security and protection, while American almanacs go further and state their appearance in a dream points to an inheritance. An Indian source adds that to see a single grandparent presages a sudden death in the family.

GRAPES
Curiously, to dream of a vineyard full of grapes is an omen of a long life, but actually to eat the fruit presages hardship. The Romans first listed dreams of grapes, and believed that if the grapes were white the dreamer could expect victory

over enemies, while the black variety signified a period of hardship. The wine growing countries of Europe such as France, Germany, Spain and Italy also have their own lore, generally agreeing that to see them growing in profusion, being harvested, or pressed into wine, points to a comfortable future. In the same nations, poor crops indicate a loss of money. In Australia, for a young woman to dream of grapes means she can expect to meet a passionate lover; in Britain it is suggested the same dream is a warning against becoming preoccupied with sensual pleasures!

GRASS
Grass is, perhaps, an unlikely element to feature in dreams, but certainly in Europe the sight of green fields of flourishing grass is an omen of good fortune — in particular advancement at work and a happy love life. Conversely, withered grass indicates months of toil for the dreamer to achieve his or her ambitions. Very long grass is said by British authorities to presage illness or bad news, while to dream of cutting grass points to a long life. An American almanac reports that to dream of eating grass symbolises repressed sexual fantasies.

GRAVE
The image of the grave has been a part of dream lore since records began, and the omens are universally unhappy. The ancient Greeks declared that a vision of an open grave presaged bad news from afar, while the Romans believed that a newly-made grave indicated the dreamer was going to suffer from the actions of others. In the Middle Ages to see a body in a grave pointed to a loss of money or property. Throughout Europe a dream of digging a grave is a sign that a special project or ambition is doomed to failure. Neglected graves are seen as indicating heartache, and for the dreamer to walk over a grave means an unhappy married life. The woman who dreams of being alone at night, in a graveyard, can expect the loss of a loved one.

GREYHOUND

The Victorians first noted the greyhound as a dream omen, and to imagine owning one was said to indicate the dreamer would increase his or her circle of friends. Almanacs of the period also noted that to see a greyhound with a female pointed to an inheritance. Today, to observe a greyhound racing is considered a gentle caution against being too hasty in any current activity; though if the animal is standing still or walking slowly, then success will crown these plans.

GUITAR

Spanish sources have for several centuries considered the guitar an omen of good luck, and believe that to dream of playing the instrument indicates happy times ahead and a new love-affair. Only if the guitar is broken will events prove disappointing. In America, however, should a dreamer imagine a guitarist being interrupted, they must beware of being cheated by friends; while if a young woman dreams of hearing a guitar, although she cannot actually see it, then she is about to be seduced by flattering words. A man who has a similar dream can also expect to fall under the dangerous spell of a seductive woman.

GUN

Some recent sources have been suggesting the gun either symbolises the dreamer's combative spirit or is another sex symbol. But, authorities over the past 200 years have been convinced it is an omen of future problems. In Europe, to dream of being shot by a gun indicates a serious illness, while to shoot someone else means a loved one is about to die. To watch while others are shot also presages a bout of poor health, though in America this dream is explained as meaning a law suit is imminent. A British almanac has also claimed that a married woman who dreams of shooting is about to face unhappiness because of another woman.

GYPSY

Dreams about gypsies are widely reported in Europe although the omens are mixed. To dream of a group of gypsies prophesies a period of restlessness, while to make any kind of deal with them — such as buying or selling merchandise — signifies good luck, though only if the transaction has been made with fairness on both sides. The Victorians believed that for a young girl to dream of having her fortune told by a gypsy would lead to a hasty and unwise marriage; and in the case of a married woman she would become unduly jealous of her husband.

H

HAIR

There is a whole variety of interpretations for dreams about hair, but the consensus of opinion indicates that full and luxuriant hair points to good health and financial stability; but thinning, unkempt or greying hair indicates carelessness in personal matters. In the Middle Ages, for a person to dream of brushing his or her hair presaged a request for help, though modern sources suggest that it prophesies a solution is about to be found to an urgent problem. For a man to dream of having his hair cut should encourage him to pursue any current ambitions as they will succeed, while a woman who dreams of having her hair styled can expect a new love-affair or an improvement in her married life. The French claim a dream of having a different colour of hair is a subconscious warning to the dreamer against telling lies; and in Britain, to dream of hair turning instantly white predicts a sudden illness or accident.

HALLWAY

The long and tortuous hallways of old castles inspired these dreams and are generally accepted to be omens of difficulties. The longer the hallway the more difficult the problems that lie ahead, though if the passage is high and beautifully decorated it will eventually bring changes for the better. American sources add that for a dreamer to meet a stranger in the hallway means he or she should beware of deceptive advice from supposed friends.

HAM
Dreams of joints of ham have been regarded throughout Europe, for at least 300 years, as omens of prosperity and good health. To imagine slicing ham denotes an ability to overcome current problems; while eating it points to some successful business dealings. Although American sources claim that a dream of broiling ham presages an important and very beneficial future event, they equally state that to imagine serving it to others will lead to family quarrels.

HANDBAG
That most cherished of a woman's possessions, her handbag, has apparently featured with increasing regularity in dreams, according to surveys on both sides of the Atlantic. The omens show that it is both an obstacle and a contrary dream. To lose a handbag presages bad luck unless it is recovered before awaking. To find a handbag complete with its contents means the dreamer can expect financial losses, while an empty bag points to some excellent business dealings. The colour of the handbag also has some bearing according to American authorities: a black bag symbolises unhappiness, a blue one happiness, and it's red for sexual satisfaction!

HANDKERCHIEF
The first Elizabethans took a great interest in dreams about handkerchiefs and declared that they symbolised flirtation and love-affairs. A torn handkerchief was said to presage trouble between lovers, while a lost one meant a broken engagement. Modern sources have seen little reason to change these omens, though it has been added that a dirty or bloodied handkerchief indicates a family quarrel, and to dream of buying handkerchiefs is a caution against a new business venture. Curiously, in Britain, for a person to

blow his or her nose during a dream signifies a better social life and new friends. In Europe, a girl who dreams of waving a handkerchief at others is being warned against a secret assignation with a man, which could lead to serious complications.

HANDS
The most basic omens concerning hands relate to their condition in the dream: if dirty or bloodied, then financial and personal problems are looming, especially in the family; but if clean, then success and happiness beckon. From the times when criminals had their hands removed as a punishment comes the omen that a severed hand presages loneliness, and to suffer burns on the hand is a warning against overstretching abilities to obtain specific objectives. To dream of washing hands points to the need to right a past wrong — according to European sources — while to dream of breaking a hand is a subconscious demand to pay closer attention to personal affairs. A recent British authority states that any dream featuring hands is an encouragement to the dreamer not to undervalue his or her work. The French have an amusing definition for lovers in this context: a dream of big hands means the person is a passionate lover, while small hands are a sign of infidelity. To dream of shaking hands with another person prophesies some unexpected good news.

HARBOUR
Another dream featured extensively in maritime almanacs because of its special omens for seafarers. A harbour without ships is understandably a bad omen of unhappy times for the family. To dream of sailing into a busy harbour indicates peace of mind and security, though to be leaving one suggests the discovery of a false friend. In Europe, it is said that to be in a harbour with family or friends presages financial gains, and to imagine a harbour in a foreign country points to some good news being on the way.

HARP

The Irish have a rich source of dream lore about the harp which has stood the test of many centuries. The omens surrounding the instrument are in the main good, indicating a happy family life; though to see one broken or with a missing string, will require strength of character to overcome a forthcoming problem of personal health, or in dealings with members of the opposite sex. To dream of playing the harp presages a new love-affair, but to see a group of people playing harps is a warning against expensive indulgences.

HARVEST

Dreams of the harvest, with all its implications for humanity, are of very ancient origin with the omens being largely predictable. Seeing an abundant harvest pointed to prosperity and happiness, while anything less was a cause for anxiety. From the Middle Ages, those who were less involved in agriculture began to read such dreams as a pointer to their own lives: a vision of men working at harvesting indicating good profits for business, while a barren harvest was said to presage troubles in love. Modern authorities state that any dream of a plentiful harvest is a sign of success for deeply-held ambitions, but a poor harvest is a warning to be on guard against exploitive friends or associates.

HAT

A dream of a new hat is a good omen for both men and women: a man can expect some advantageous changes in business, while a woman is going to attract some new admirers. Losing a hat is quite a different matter; as a man will suffer some loss of business, and a woman may well experience sexual problems. To dream of wearing an old hat is a sign of poverty; a hat that is too large will cause embarrassment; and one that is too small prophesies a disappointment. American sources add that to dream of wearing a big or elaborate hat indicates prosperity, but a straw hat is a sign of conceit.

HATRED
Not a pleasant emotion, but one recorded in many dreams over the years. Most authorities agree that to dream of hating someone is a warning against misjudging others, for such hatred translated into real life can rebound on the dreamer. On the other hand, to imagine being the object of hatred actually points to finding a number of caring and obliging friends who will help the dreamer through forthcoming problems. A recent American source adds two further omens to the list: to hate enemies will result in winning a lawsuit; and to dream of hating relatives promises happiness in domestic affairs.

HEALTH
Concern with health has led to considerable interest in dreams about this subject and most authorities agree that if the symptoms appear bad, the omens in real life are good. For example, to imagine being in poor health presages some pleasant events to come, although a breakdown in health should be read as a warning against any unnecessary speculation. A European source claims that to dream of recovering from poor health, suggests greater trust in the advice of family and friends; while an Australian almanac recently defined a dream in which children appeared to be in bad health as a sign of forthcoming prosperity.

HEARSE
Like health, this is a dream of contrary, for instead of the omens predicting doom, the sight of a hearse promises the end of some persistent worry. Even in the sixteenth century, when the hearse carrying bodies to the graveyard was an everyday occurrence, dream lore had this vision marked down as indicating happiness for the dreamer. More recently, to take a ride in a hearse has been described as

presaging important but beneficial changes in life; and only a dream of a military hearse is believed to be ill-omened and convey the likelihood of emotional sorrow, according to American authorities.

HEART
Matters of the heart engaged the attention of many nineteenth-century dream researchers, one of their most vivid pronouncements declaring that any pain in the heart pointed to trouble in business. For a young woman to dream of her heart — or any heart-shaped object, for that matter — presaged a love-affair. Nowadays, any dream of suffering a heart attack is considered a vision of contrary and points to a long and happy life. In Europe, to dream of seeing a living heart was said to prophesy that a lack of energy would be followed by sickness; while in America recent books of dream lore have described the feeling of being heartless as a sure sign of success in business.

HEATHER
The Scots consider a dream of heather to be very lucky, particularly for the dreamer's personal life and relationships. Since the fourteenth century, white heather has been considered an especially good omen, promising the dreamer a caring and devoted partner. Several authorities also believe the luck is enhanced still more if the heather was seen growing wild and the sun was shining upon it.

HEDGEROWS
A dream much commoner among women than men, where the state of the hedgerow is crucial. A flourishing hedge is a sign of love and happiness, though one which is bare or covered in thorns points to domestic problems. Victorian almanacs declared that a young woman who dreamed of walking beside a hedge with her lover would soon be married, though if either of them became entangled with the hedge their life together would be beset by quarrels. For

men, to dream of clipping a hedgerow is an omen of satisfactory business dealings, say several British authorities,
but to pass through a gap in one could lead to the embarrassing end of a love-affair.

HEIRLOOM

The seventeenth century saw the first extensive recording
of dreams about heirlooms, and the recognition that the
omens concerning them were mixed. A German authority
claimed that to inherit an heirloom put the dreamer in
danger of losing what he already possessed unless he or
she lived up to their responsibilities. In America, a dream of
receiving a piece of family property was seen as indicating
family quarrels, and that the recipient was in further
danger of becoming dominated by avaricious friends. This
century, in Britain, the dream has become more widely
accepted to symbolise the achievement of respect in personal and business life.

HELL

The concept of hell, as a domain of evil, has been established since the earliest times, and for centuries dreams
about the place were said to be symbolic of temptation. If
the dreamer allowed himself to be bewitched by the
'pleasures of hell' he could expect financial and moral disaster, claimed the old almanacs. In the Middle Ages,
however, to see people in hell pointed to a long life, but to
talk with them, however briefly, warned of being ensnared
by enemies. Today, any vision which can be equated with
the classical idea of hell is said to presage a rise in financial
benefits, but a comparative fall in social popularity.

HERBS

European almanacs have for several hundred years attributed the happiest omens to herbs, believing them to
symbolise good health and peace of mind. In Britain, a
dream of a flourishing herb garden indicates to the dreamer

he or she is much admired and can expect success in business and personal relationships. Several Far Eastern sources believe that if the herbs are flowering then travel is forecast; while in America to dream of cutting the plants for use, indicates a long life. A French authority has also written recently that the dream may be suggesting the use of alternative medicines, if normal medication is failing to cure an illness.

HERO

To dream of being a hero can occupy daytime hours as well as sleep, but according to dream lore the night vision works in reverse. If a person dreams of being a hero, they can expect some sharp criticism from authority, but if they see someone else being a hero, then the omens indicate the successful solution to a long-standing business problem. An American source has suggested that to be a witness to a heroic action is an indication that someone who has been bearing the dreamer a grudge is about to have a change of heart. A Swedish dream researcher has added that the dream may be symbolic of certain powers within the dreamer, of which they are either aware or have not yet ventured to try.

HIDING

The sensation of hiding oneself is well known in dream lore, and in fact is often listed as being among the most common of recurring dreams. For many years it has been seen as symbolising that the dreamer is avoiding facing up to problems in life and ought to seek help. To dream of hiding specific items is also indicative of being secretive when openness with family or friends is what is really needed. According to a recent American source, to see other people hiding means the dreamer is being deceived; while to discover something that has been hidden is a sign of unexpected pleasures.

HILLS

All the authorities are agreed that to dream of climbing up a hill leads to good fortune, though to fail to reach the top presages a certain amount of aggravation among acquaintances. The higher the hill, the better the luck, European sources say — adding the proviso that if the climb seems very exhausting the happiness will be tempered with a little sorrow. If members of the family also take part in the climb, then, a Russian authority adds, the dreamer will soon enjoy a little financial windfall.

HISTORY

The ancient civilisations of Rome and Greece were both very interested in their past glories, and dreams of history are first noted from these periods. Both nations were agreed that any dreams which featured historic occasions or personalities were symbolic of new opportunities for the dreamer's personal advancement. This definition has remained unchanged through the centuries. In Europe, later authorities have said that a dream of studying history books points to a long and pleasant recreation; while American sources have suggested that this could also be a warning about being told lies by friends or acquaintances.

HOBBIES

Dreaming about a hobby, whether it is a current interest or one the dreamer would like to indulge in, is seen as symbolic of the need for a change; in particular a rest from demanding work. The Victorians, who first began to pursue hobbies with enthusiasm, interpreted these dreams as predicting changes in life, though any changes would not be achieved without some difficulty. It is a good omen to dream of children pursuing their hobbies, as several European sources believe this indicates some profitable dealings in the future.

HOE
Rural almanacs have for generations stated that hoes are symbolic of freedom from want, and to dream of working with a hoe presages a secure if hard-working future. These same books claimed that a woman who dreamed of hoeing was of an independent nature, and well able to support herself; while any lovers who saw the same vision could count on the constancy of their partners. Today, the dream is universally seen as pointing to improved prospects in the future.

HOLE
The dream of falling into a hole is another sensation reported since before biblical times, and defined quite simply as prophesying illness. To dream of making a hole points to going on a long journey, while to step into a hole is a warning about making undesirable friends. Throughout Europe, to dream of seeing a hole in any item of clothing is believed to indicate an improvement in the dreamer's financial matters.

HOLIDAY
The idea of a holiday, as distinct from travel, has only entered dream lore during this century. Authorities believe that to imagine being on holiday foretells meeting some interesting strangers whose company the dreamer will enjoy. A British source has suggested that the dream is actually an encouragement to work harder to achieve current objectives; while a German almanac says that a girl who dreams of not enjoying herself on holiday is 'secretly worrying about losing her lover to another woman'.

HOME
As the centre of most people's lives, the home is a good omen, presaging a period of happy family life as long as everything is bright and well-ordered. Some almanacs state that to dream of visiting the old family home indicates some

good news is on the way — unless it has been allowed to fall into disrepair, as this points to the sickness or death of a relative. In America, to dream of renovating a home symbolises a secure future, though curiously, the same authorities state that to see a home on fire means an inheritance! A variation of this dream, reported from South America, says that to dream of a home being shaken by an earthquake is a sign of losing money. To dream of losing a home is a warning that the dreamer is about to lose faith in the integrity of other people. A recent study has further suggested that to dream of home while living away is a sign that return visits should be made more often.

HOMOSEXUAL
A recent British study has suggested that for any heterosexual person to dream about homosexuals may be symbolic of a basic insecurity about their relationships with the opposite sex, and has advised seeking psychological guidance. In several American books of dream lore, however, such dreams are said to have good omens: seeing homosexuals points to financial gain, and actually meeting a group of them is indicative of recovering some lost money.

HONEY
Another very ancient dream with good omens, for honey is believed to be symbolic of love and wealth. The earliest almanacs claimed that to dream of eating honey predicted domestic and social happiness, and for lovers it was a sign that they would shortly be getting married. To dream of collecting honey points to financial gains, and several European sources add that a dreamer who imagines giving honey to other people will soon hear good news of a person close to them who has been ill or in some kind of trouble.

HOODS
To see a hooded figure in a dream, whether it is the dreamer in person, or someone else, is a warning to guard against

being deceived, say European authorities. For several centuries hooded monks were the subject of many dreams, and old almanacs instructed the dreamer to watch out for people who might seem to be friends, but were actually plotting harm. French dream lore says that a young woman who dreams of wearing a hood is subconsciously planning to seduce a married man.

HORSE
The Romans and Arabs had an extensive dream lore about horses which, of course, were vital to their well-being. The ancient civilisations believed the horse to be symbolic of prosperity, and dreams of riding a horse — especially a white one — pointed to a contented future and good relations with family and friends. To see horses running in a dream indicates success with ambitions, though an injured or dead horse is an omen of illness in the family. The Italians believe a man who dreams of himself on a bay horse will enjoy a new and passionate love-affair; while a woman who dreams of a black horse is being warned that her husband is unfaithful. The Spanish say to dream of being thrown or kicked by a horse points to being spurned by a loved one and losing money — probably through a business venture. A dream of horses has recently been described as another subconscious expression of a desire for freedom, and a feeling that aspirations and objectives are not being realised.

HOSPITAL
The earliest dreams of being a patient in a hospital are to be found in the middle of the nineteenth century, and indicate that our ancestors believed these were warnings of a contagious disease in their community which they should avoid at all costs. If the dreamer was visiting a patient in the hospital he or she could expect bad news of an absent friend or relative. Today most authorities agree these dreams signify the dreamer is overworking or worrying too much, and

should seek the help of others immediately. A curious American almanac claims that to dream of being in a mental hospital is a warning to control sexual urges.

HOTEL
The Victorians believed dreams of staying in a hotel signi-fied a life of contentment and profit; but modern authorities are inclined to the view this is a dream of contrary, and the more ostentatious and grand the hotel the bigger the dis-appointment that will greet the outcome of a cherished project. To be alone in a hotel, or with a member of the opposite sex, points to problems in domestic affairs — although not necessarily in America, where several books of dream lore claim the man who dreams of being in a hotel with his lover is about to become wealthy. The same books also say a dream of going to live in a hotel will result in the solving of a mystery that has been puzzling the dreamer. European sources further suggest that to dream of being a hotel owner presages making a fortune.

HOUNDS
Bloodhounds have a long association with sex in dream lore. To dream of hunting with hounds has, for several centuries, been said to indicate that the dreamer will have lots of admirers, though these people will feel no real love for him or her. The Victorians said a woman who dreamed of bloodhounds would fall in love with 'a man below her station'; while a man who had the same experience would be unable to resist 'consorting with fallen women'. Today's sources agree that a dream of being chased by hounds is telling the dreamer he or she should be more restrained in sensual pleasures.

HOUSE
Because much of family life takes place in the house, dreams about them have been described since Roman times as being symbolic of the dreamer's own social, family and

intimate life. Although Freud believed the house had a female symbolism (and other dream researchers have suggested that each floor of the building represents a different area of the body), the consensus of modern opinion still shares the original Roman concept that the omens relate to the dreamer's relationships with his family and friends, as well as his attitude towards himself. In other words, what is seen of the house, either inside or out, plus the atmosphere and condition, can be related to what the future holds.

HUNCHBACK
The omens about hunchbacks are strangely varied in different parts of the world. In much of Europe to dream of a hunchback was said to signify a sudden reverse in the dreamer's prospects, and to imagine being one indicated that a terrible humiliation was about to fall upon the dreamer. In both Britain and America, however, these unfortunate people are nowadays regarded as dream omens of good luck. An Australian almanac has further claimed that to dream of talking to a hunchback is a pointer to a happy love-affair.

HURDLES
To try to overcome hurdles, in any shape or form, is another of the classic obstacle dreams. Struggling to get over the hurdles is symbolic of a number of suspicions which are affecting the dreamer's personal happiness and prospects, and only if the barriers are cleared can he or she expect to enjoy a contented life once again. Honesty with those involved in the suspicions is being called for to resolve this situation.

HURRICANE
Another terrifying dream which has been recorded from the earliest times, and one which presages problems in life unless a very serious change in attitude towards others is contemplated. To see a hurricane was said by American

almanacs to threaten a collapse in business, although in Europe it signified an unexpected family removal. A recent study of the dream has concluded that it is symbolic of being overwhelmed by feelings of inadequacy, and that counselling should be sought.

I

ICE

Scandinavian folklore has a lot to say about dreams of ice, and along with other sources proves it to be one more instance of contrary. For example, to imagine being on ice indicates a sound future ahead, and even to break through it is confirmation that the dreamer is worrying unnecessarily about a current problem. European authorities accept these definitions, too, adding that to see a vast expanse of ice is symbolic of some good business deals, although to imagine sheets of ice (including an iceberg) floating on water is a hint that some plans are going to be disrupted by ill-disposed associates. An American almanac claims that to dream of running on ice prophesies deception in love, while a recent book of Swiss dream lore reports that ice-skating with a partner is a warning against indiscriminate sexual relations.

ICE-CREAM

Just as eating ice-cream is a pleasure, so dreams about it foretell good luck. European almanacs claim it signifies success in any venture being undertaken, and American sources add that to see others eating ice-cream — in particular children — denotes prosperity and happiness. A woman who dreams of spilling ice-cream, however, is about to be flirted with; and seemingly the only bad omen concerns melted ice-cream which presages stagnation in some eagerly awaited pleasures.

IDOLS
Dreams about idols can be found in the earliest collections of folklore. The first authorities believed that any dream of worshipping an idol pointed to the dreamer allowing petty things to tyrannise them, and would therefore hold up their progress to wealth and fame; while to smash an idol was symbolic of mastery over self. Christian sources later declared that to imagine idolising a saint pointed to the dreamer being much loved by family and friends. Recently, it has been suggested these experiences indicate the dreamer is placing too much reliance on the opinions of others — not always wisely. Alternatively, it is a prediction that the dreamer is about to discover a secret of considerable significance in his or her life.

ILLNESS
Another of those dreams which frequently proves uncannily true. Although it is not always the dreamer who falls sick, even if he or she imagines being in poor health, it can just as well be any member of the immediate family. Authorities have always advised seeking medical guidance after such a dream, especially where women are concerned, for the omens suggest that the illness will be accompanied by a deep feeling of depression. A recent American almanac of romance claims a dream of illness will spell the end of a love-affair, and that to visualise a partner being ill is a warning of 'foregoing some anticipated pleasure'.

IMPALED
The omens for a dream of being impaled or caught on a hook in any way can be traced back to the Middle Ages where such cruelty and torture was deliberately practised in many societies. Sources then declared it to be a warning to be on the look-out for threats from enemies, and only if

the dreamer escaped before waking could he be sure of avoiding the danger. Today the dream is seen as symbolising a difficult situation which threatens the dreamer unless he can extricate himself by force of character. To see others impaled is a similar warning of troubled times ahead.

IMPOTENCE
Dreams of sexual impotence have certainly been experienced for many centuries, although they are not widely recorded despite the authorities being agreed that this is a dream of opposite effect. European sources were the first to declare that to imagine being impotent presaged a full and vigorous sex life; while in Britain the more reserved Victorian almanacs confided to their male readers that the sensation actually prophesied unexpected wealth. Turn-of-the-century American sources also claimed the dream implied receiving a legacy.

IMPRISONED
A fear that invaded the dreams of the earliest communities, and was originally defined as a warning to be on guard against treachery. From the eighteenth century it came to be regarded as a caution against mixing with criminals or people of base instincts, although some European sources felt it was indicative of an unhappy marriage. Modern authorities, however, believe it to be symbolic of tension and strain, probably brought on by extravagance; although in the case of a woman the cause may be an affair which she is keeping secret from her husband or regular partner.

INCEST
An unpleasant dream which has caused much heart-searching among those who have admitted to the experience. Authorities are agreed that the dream does not symbolise the act itself, but rather an unconscious fear of a discreditable action. For instance, a British book of dream

lore, published in the 1920s, told its readers: 'To dream of incestuous practices denotes you will fall from honourable places and will also suffer loss in business.' A recent dream study, published in America, underlined the importance of resisting the pressures being placed upon the subject, as implied by the dream, as the consequences of giving in could be disastrous.

INCOHERENT
Incoherent dreams, in which people seem to be moving in slow motion, and in which their speech is quite unintelligible, are widely believed to be ill-omened. A century ago, almanacs defined such experiences as the result of a series of changing events in the dreamer's life, which had brought about exhaustion and nervousness. Recent British and American studies of this type of dream, however, believe its explanation is far simpler — the dreamer is afraid of some hidden secret being made public.

INCOME TAX
The payment of income tax is described often enough in life as a nightmare, but actually to dream of facing this situation has various omens. In Britain, several authorities claim the experience presages the non-arrival of an expected payment, while in America a dream of being unable to pay income tax is a forecast of monetary losses. A French book of dream lore notes, somewhat tongue-in-cheek, that to dream of paying income tax is a sign of having mean relatives! But, across the border in Germany, another authority claims that to have the happy experience of getting a refund of income tax points to a major success in business.

INDECENT
Any act of indecency in a dream is said to be a warning to the dreamer to watch his or her manners and temper. The genteel almanacs of the seventeenth century informed readers that to dream of wearing unduly revealing clothes,

to use bad language, or to behave in an indecent way, presaged social disgrace. A recent American source has reported that, for a man, a dream of indecency is telling him he lives only for business; while a woman will experience several unhappy love-affairs. A bizarre Spanish book of dream lore has suggested that to be put in jail for indecency foretells great accomplishments in business dealings!

INFIDELITY
The Victorian books of dream lore took a high moral tone with any female readers who dreamed of straying outside their marriage for sexual pleasures, and insisted the lady would soon find herself the subject of unfavourable comment; a man, too, could expect to be ostracised by his friends. A less severe tone has been taken in a recent American study, which accepts the dream may well be an accurate reflection of the subject's life but recommends greater discretion in the choice of partners because of the dangers of promiscuous sex.

INHERITANCE
The omens for this dream are reported as being quite contrary on opposite sides of the Atlantic. In Britain, the dream of inheriting money or property has for centuries been seen as a pointer to receiving an actual legacy; while throughout the rest of Europe it is considered to be an indication of ambitions being realised — though perhaps not on quite the scale that is desired. But in America the dreamer can expect only a death in the family.

INJURY
Dreamers who imagined themselves being injured were comforted, for a great many years, by the interpretation that this was a dream of contrary and that the omens for the future were generally good for both health and welfare. In the Far East, to dream of injuring someone else was a caution to beware of false friends; while European sources

have suggested that a man who imagined himself being injured by another male would soon have a rival in love. A recent British report has, however, concluded that the dream is symbolic of carelessness, and that the dreamer should take warning from this before any real problems are encountered.

INK
The ink blot has been a part of dream lore for several centuries, one of the most popular definitions claiming that it signifies the dreamer's love is not being reciprocated. Other sources have suggested that the blot presages a period of unhappiness, more specifically a number of family quarrels. Victorian almanacs believed that ink spilled on clothes was a warning to beware of small acts of meanness and that smears on the fingers were a sign of a jealous nature. The omens were worse if the ink was red. Today, dreaming of writing a letter with ink is said, by virtually all authorities, to presage a time of happiness.

INSANITY
Our forebears believed dreams of insanity to be very ill-omened, but since the end of the Victorian era they have been considered experiences of contrary. Earlier generations felt that work and health would be seriously affected by dreaming of being insane, and that to see a group of mad people would put a severe strain on financial resources. Modern authorities feel that good news can be expected after this dream, especially in money matters; if other insane people are involved in the dream, current plans will still succeed, but the success could be tempered by a problem or two.

INSCRIPTIONS
Interestingly, in the vast majority of cases of dreams about inscriptions — such as those on monuments, buildings or graves — the dreamers have been unable to remember the

precise nature of the wording. The authorities are agreed, however, that the essential element is the object upon which the inscription is written: on a statue it signifies an award, on a building a change of residence, and on a tombstone a happy event such as a wedding or a birth! Should it be possible to read the inscription, says a British source, this indicates that the dreamer will be able to solve whatever problems are causing anxiety.

INSULT
Books of dream lore from earlier days were much concerned about the experience of being insulted, as the significance of this mattered greatly in the lives of the gentry and the nobility. In Britain, the dream was listed as one of contrary — it signified the dreamer had friends who could be relied upon — and so it has remained to this day. Throughout much of Europe, the dreamer was being warned against foolish actions, while in Russia and China the omens indicated trouble ahead. In both these countries, however, to dream of insulting enemies was felt to prophesy good fortune.

INTERCOURSE
Open references to dreams of having sex are rarely to be found in almanacs until the middle of the twentieth century, although euphemisms for the act were sometimes slipped in under the headings of love or romance. Undoubtedly, though, men and women have always dreamed of copulating and the omens of such dreams have predictably been related to whether or not the couple were married. Modern authorities believe that for any dreamer to imagine participating in intercourse is synonymous with a contented lifestyle, unless the experience was somehow distasteful or unpleasant. To dream of watching other couples having sex is a pointer to some personal problem about which medical advice should be sought.

INTOXICATION

The Romans believed a dream of being intoxicated was a good omen, as it resulted from imbibing the nectar of the gods. Later generations tended to be much more disapproving of the sensation as they felt it presaged a dissolute life. From the eighteenth century onwards, the dream was said to symbolise the dreamer's desire for 'illicit pleasures', though in some European countries there was a feeling it represented a desire for knowledge which other people would consider foolish. Today's authorities have stated that it is a warning against too much high living, while an American source adds that it can also presage financial troubles.

INVENTOR

To dream of being an inventor or of creating something new for science or industry has, since the Industrial Revolution, been looked upon as a good omen. The experience is very much one of aspiration, and even to dream of other people creating inventions, or perhaps meeting real inventors, still hints at striving to achieve the highest ambitions. It is a particularly good omen to see children working at inventions, states an American source. Most authorities who have studied this particular dream, however, feel compelled to report that few dreamers can remember anything specific about their 'great invention'!

INVITATION

To receive an invitation in a dream is not at all what it seems, for it presages some bad news, according to most authorities. The Europeans believe that if the invitation is to travel, a period of boredom will follow; while the Americans say an invitation to a party will cause problems at work. To dream of a dinner invitation will also be followed by a time of very few social engagements. Conversely, to imagine inviting a famous person to dinner is an omen of financial gains — according to a British almanac. In America

113

the same thing will result in a long-standing problem being solved.

ISLANDS
Islands have always symbolised peace and contentment, and likewise in dreams they have been seen as omens of happiness and good living. Of late, researchers have questioned this *blanket* approval and suggested that the person who dreams of being on an island may be suffering from problems of conscience involving some recent activity. Certainly, anyone who imagines being a castaway on an island is in for a hard time in social and domestic matters, unless he quits the island before awakening. To see a beautiful island from a distance signifies travel; while an island that appears to be heavily populated is an indicator to the dreamer of a hard struggle to make good in life. Another British source has also suggested the dream is urging the subject to be more outgoing and trusting, and not keep to himself.

IVY
Since the Middle Ages, ivy has been synonymous in dreams with good health and financial security — especially when the climbing plant is growing on a house. If the ivy is very profuse, the dreamer will have lots of loyal friends, and if it is seen climbing up trees then a long and vigorous life is predicted. By contrast, some romantic almanacs of the nineteenth century claimed that a man who dreamed he saw ivy growing up a wall in the moonlight would suffer a broken engagement; while a young lady undergoing the same experience could expect to have a number of clandestine meetings with men.

J

JACKDAW

The omens surrounding a jackdaw in a dream are curiously mixed. For centuries, throughout Europe, the bird has been seen as symbolising sickness and family disputes, yet it can also signify happiness in love. The bad omens appear to be when the bird is visualised on the wing, but for a girl to dream of catching one indicates she will soon be married. A man who does the same can expect to outwit his rivals in matters of love. A French almanac also notes that to imagine killing a jackdaw will cause the dreamer to inherit some property.

JACKPOT

Dreams of winning a jackpot seem to be peculiarly American, and the published authorities declare it to be a case of contrary. The dream signifies a period of hard work for little reward, although if the prize was won by someone else a small inheritance can be expected.

JAIL

The threat of prison has caused it to be another topic well represented in the dream lore of most countries. For generations, to imagine being imprisoned was taken as a sign of a hard life, and writers were at pains to urge their readers to avoid a life of crime. Women who dreamed of their menfolk in jail were told they would have to endure much suffering; while a young girl who saw her lover in jail was being warned about his suspect character. Nowadays, European sources believe this to be an obstacle dream: the subject's problem will be short-lived if he or she escapes before awakening. To see other people in jail indicates freedom from worry, according to a British authority; while an American almanac recently claimed, rather strangely, that to dream of being in jail would result in 'public esteem'.

JAM
This popular preserve has a happy reputation in dream lore, and there is a remarkably large number of experiences on record in which jam features. It is said to be symbolic of domestic happiness, and for a woman to dream of making jam foretells she will have a happy home and lots of appreciative friends. Throughout Europe, to dream of eating jam signifies a surprise — most probably an unexpected journey to be reunited with an old friend.

JARS
Stone jars, which were a feature of Roman life, found their way into dream lore at about that period of history and were soon defined as omens of good fortune, particularly for the elderly. However, the jar had to be full, for empty vessels were symbolic of poverty and unhappiness. Broken jars have also been described as omens of sickness. In recent times, any jar of preserves is believed to signify a happy social life — according to a British source — while in America, a jar of candy is said to lead to problems just melting away!

JAWS
The threatening jaws of wild beasts are another element in dreams that can be traced back to the oldest documents, where they are believed to warn that enemies were plotting against the dreamer. In the Middle Ages, any dream of

116

deformed jaws was said to be a caution about business dealings, while an injury to a jaw indicated there would be disagreements among friends. Modern authorities have stated that a dreamer who experiences pain in the jaw is the subject of malicious gossip; while to be threatened by jaws of any kind now signifies problems of a financial nature.

JEALOUSY
The romantic almanacs define dreams of jealousy as ill-omened, and from the seventeenth century they were said to presage bad news concerning marriage relationships or love-affairs. Dream lore maintains that for a husband to be jealous of his wife is a warning about being cautious in all his dealings; while for a wife it indicates a series of vexing events. For a lover to be jealous of his partner points to a rival in love. Modern research also suggests that this dream could well be a warning against too much self-indulgence.

JESUS CHRIST
Dreams of the figure of Jesus have been recorded since the advent of Christianity, and are believed to be symbolic of consolation and fortitude being promised to the dreamer, in preparation for some testing times that lie ahead. In the Middle Ages, dreams in which Christ appeared to speak were reported from all over Europe and were said to be promises of peace of mind. To imagine talking to Christ has also been claimed, by several American religious publications, to be a hint about making charity donations to the poor.

JEWELLERY
A whole catalogue of definitions could be offered about the omens relating to the various kinds of jewellery, but there is actually very little difference between them. The Romans first declared jewellery to be an omen of good fortune as long as it was being given or received; to imagine wearing an ostentatious display of precious stones was, though, a

warning against impulsive behaviour and becoming a prey to vanity. German sources noted that broken jewellery was a sign of a broken friendship or love-affair, and that to dream of buying jewels presaged an accident. Victorian almanacs warned their young female readers that a dream of losing jewellery meant they ran the risk of meeting a smooth-tongued young man who would flatter to deceive. Modern sources believe all omens about loss depend on whether the item is recovered before awaking.

JILTED
For either sex to imagine being jilted by someone they love would seem an unhappy dream, but the omens are actually quite the reverse and indicate success in courting and marriage! The French believe that a woman who dreams of jilting a man is frivolous by nature, while an unmarried man who imagines himself being spurned — whether he has proposed marriage or not — can look forward to good luck with other women. A recent American book of dream lore suggests that a married woman who dreams of jilting a secret lover is actually concerned about her sex drive.

JOB
Having a job is a concern for many men and women, and research has found it an increasingly recurring feature in dreams in the past 50 years. The consensus of opinion, however, is that this is a dream of contrary and to imagine losing a job is actually a pointer to being offered promotion or even a change to a new and better position. Conversely, being offered promotion is a subtle warning to put in more effort at work, while to imagine offering work to others is a hint about becoming over-confident.

JOCKEY
The omens about jockeys in dreams vary around the world. In America, for example, a winning jockey is said to symbolise easy money, while a loser warns the dreamer to

beware of being cheated by friends. British authorities maintain that a woman who dreams of a jockey will get an unexpected proposal of marriage, although a man is being warned to control his passions. In Australia, a jockey signifies a surprise gift, but to dream of a jockey being thrown from a horse points to the dreamer being approached by a stranger for a loan.

JOURNEY
Dreams of making a journey are a long-established tradition, with some of the first being reported in the Arab world. The dream is widely said to be symbolic of a change in circumstances, though whether for the better or worse depends on the nature of the journey. If the experience is pleasant, then the future looks profitable, though any form of accident presages trouble in family life. A journey on foot indicates a hard slog to success, but the faster the means of transport the quicker the dreamer will accomplish a current ambition. Several European sources claim that to dream of bad weather on a journey is a warning to take care in personal matters, and to imagine carrying weapons is symbolic of getting married. Any journey with children is said by a British source to be a good omen.

JUDGE
Judges have been omens of bad luck for at least 400 years and are said to symbolise sorrow and unhappiness. European authorities believe that any experience in which the dreamer see a judge, or appears to be one, points to hard times; though the view is tempered in America by claims that the problems will be temporary. In the East, a dream in which the judge acquits a defendant is said to presage an inheritance.

JUMP
The sensation of jumping is said to be symbolic of trying to achieve success over adversity at a time when the dreamer

is oppressed with problems. The Victorians believed that if the dreamer fell back, this was an indication greater effort was required to overcome the difficulties, while to jump down from any point presaged a reckless action or a disappointment in love. American authorities recently stated that dreams of jumping are an indication the sleeper is very inconsistent in love-affairs — although to succeed in jumping over any object means some happy news is on the way. The French believe that to dream of jumping into water is a sign the dreamer is about to be persecuted.

JUNGLE
Being lost in a jungle is an unnerving dream and symbolic of becoming entangled in matters of finance or the heart. Struggling through dense undergrowth signifies wrestling with mounting debts, say European authorities, while being threatened by wild animals is a sign of having rivals for a loved one. An American source claims a jungle dream is a warning against an ill-advised romantic entanglement, and a recent British report alternatively suggested it as 'a subconscious desire to break from routine and seek new experiences'.

JURY
The eighteenth century provided the first instances of dreams about juries, when the omen was defined as promising the dreamer a change for the better in life. To serve on a jury is said to presage some kind of recognition from valued friends or associates, although European sources feel it is a rather less specific encouragement to trust more in your own judgement. An unusual American dream almanac published in the 1920s declared, rather chillingly, that to dream of being a juror meant the death of an enemy!

K

KALEIDOSCOPE

The Americans have an interesting store of omens about dreams which feature kaleidoscopes of colours and images. They are said to be symbolic of a change in life, with new friends and new experiences promising to brighten an existence that has fallen into a rut. Where the dreamer has been sober and cautious, he or she can expect to be frivolous and pleasure-seeking. To see an actual kaleidoscope is said to indicate inheriting some money.

KANGAROO

In Australia the kangaroo is regarded either as a delightful creature or as a pest, and the omens of dreaming about one are similarly diverse. To see one jumping is symbolic of taking a trip, while to be attacked by a roo means the sleeper's reputation is in danger of being sullied by scandal. An early twentieth-century almanac says the sight of a kangaroo's hide indicates imminent success for some long-standing ambition; while to kill one of the creatures presages a notable achievement despite many obstacles. A British authority has recently suggested the dream symbolises a desire to side-step crucial matters for a quiet life, when they should really be confronted.

KEEPSAKE

A keepsake or small personal gift was very welcome to young Victorian ladies, and almanacs of this period suggest such a dream augers well. The best dreams were those in which the sleeper was giving the keepsake, as this symbolised good luck and prosperity; while to receive one indicated some changes in life. Modern authorities have suggested that the giving of any keepsake comes with a warning — do not let a family argument become a major disagreement.

KETTLE

The kettle, as one of the symbols of hearth and home, has been regarded as an important topic in dreams dating from at least the sixteenth century. European sources are agreed that it symbolises hard work, but if the kettle is clean and full of water then it also assures peace and contentment. For a young girl to see a broken kettle in a dream indicated a disappointment in love, according to Victorian almanacs; while modern sources assure her counterpart today that she can look forward to a handsome and attentive lover if she dreams of an electric kettle on the boil.

KEYS

Dreams of keys have a longer tradition than might be expected, considering that for many centuries they were only to be found in castles, mansions and large houses. The most widely reported omen suggests they symbolise the unlocking of a secret, though in Europe it is stressed that the solution is most likely to be discovered if the keys were actually found by the dreamer. Naturally, bad news will follow the loss of keys, and in Asia a broken key portends a separation, or perhaps a serious illness or death. To dream of being given some keys indicates help from friends. Modern authorities also believe the key to be a sex symbol, and claim that dreams of fitting one into a keyhole presage a good sex life.

KICK

To dream of being kicked may not be brought about just by the restlessness of a partner, but because an omen, reported since the Middle Ages, says this symbolises having powerful enemies. Today, authorities have somewhat modified this definition to indicate anxiety brought about by problems in business. Curiously, in America, to imagine kicking someone else indicates financial gains.

KIDNAP

With kidnapping a comparatively common occurrence throughout Europe during the past few centuries, it is no surprise to find it firmly entrenched in dream lore. Earlier omens said it was symbolic of losing valuables or having to make an unexpected change of abode; but modern authorities feel it is more a warning about the kind of people the dreamer is associating with, and the effect they can have on his or her life. Victorian almanacs informed a single girl who dreamed of kidnap that she was in danger of becoming a flirt, while a recent American publication tells her modern counterpart it means she will soon get pregnant!

KILLING

Another of the oldest dreams on record and once again an instance of contrary: the dreamer who imagines being killed will enjoy a long life. The Greeks believed that to imagine killing a member of the family, such as a mother or father, presaged a crop failure, while to kill any wild creature denoted a victory in battle. In Europe, to witness a killing, whether of animals or human beings indicates some unhappy changes in life, though in America one source insists that killing a businessman signifies security! The consensus of opinion among modern authorities is that the dream points to the onset of a period of emotional stress, and they suggest getting medical advice.

KING

From the Middle Ages, any dream in which a king appeared was regarded as a very good omen which promised the dreamer a rise in status. In Europe, for at least two centuries, any girl who dreamed of meeting a king was said to be in danger of marrying a man she would fear; while a man who imagined himself as a king had an ambition that might well outstrip his capabilities. For a time, too, French almanacs claimed that those who dreamed of royalty would encounter deceit in love-affairs. If the dream king is seen in any kind of unpleasant situation, then modern sources say this means the dreamer will be the subject of much malicious gossip.

KISSING

A pleasant sensation, and in dream lore the omens are governed by the circumstances of the kiss. A kiss of affection to a member of the family, a lover, a relative or a friend is symbolic of happiness and success in current enterprises, but one stolen furtively will lead to sorrow. In the Middle Ages to kiss a stranger denoted loose morals, and to see an unknown person kissing a sweetheart pointed to the end of a courtship. Nowadays, to dream of kissing someone who is disliked prophesies an illness. An American source adds the unlikely footnote that for a man to dream of kissing someone's bottom means he is going to be deceived by his lover!

KITCHEN

Dreams abut the kitchen seem to be a peculiarly European and American tradition, though the omens vary on either side of the Atlantic. A clean and tidy kitchen indicates happy social events, say British sources; while in America it predicts the unexpected arrival of a friend. Throughout Europe, to see a slovenly kitchen is a warning of bad news from a family member living far away, though the Americans prefer to define this as indicating the imminent arrival of some money! The woman who dreams of seeing others working in her kitchen has a health problem and should consult a doctor, says a modern British authority.

KITTENS
Kittens were much-favoured omens in dream almanacs a century ago, because they promised young women pleasant romantic affairs. In Europe (where cats are treated less as pets and more as a means of pest control), to dream about new-born kittens is said to presage a recovery from illness. In America, the woman who sees a beautiful white kitten should beware of an artful seducer coming into her life, while any man who dreams of one is about to have a disappointing love-affair.

KNICKERS
The omens that used to be applied to dreams of pantaloons have been transferred, virtually intact, to knickers. In Europe in the eighteenth century a man's dream of a girl wearing pantaloons was said to indicate he would be lucky in love; while a woman who visualised the same thing could feel secure in her own relationship. Both British and American sources agree that to dream of knickers is now an omen of a full sexual life. The French add that the man who dreams of a woman in knickers, but with her face masked or unrecognisable, is gullible in matters of love.

KNIFE
A knife (or dagger) has been a bad omen in dreams since the times of the Romans, and though it does not symbolise death it does indicate separation and arguments among family or relatives. The sharper the knife, the bigger the worries, according to the old European almanacs. A broken knife signifies the end of a love-affair, while any closed or sheathed knife predicts trouble with the law. An American source has suggested a simple table knife symbolises an invitation to dinner; while any kind of cut inflicted

by a knife in a dream is a warning about curbing rash emotions.

KNITTING
In a woman's dream, the pleasant task of knitting is an omen of a quiet and peaceful home life. Should such thoughts intrude into a man's sleeping hours he can look forward to renewing a friendship — with a female. Victorian almanacs first warned that to drop stitches in a dream of knitting indicated a domestic row, and for a man to see himself in any kind of weaving factory signified he would lead a steady and thrifty life. Curiously, modern American sources believe that a young woman who dreams of knitting will make a hasty marriage.

KNOTS
Dreaming of knots has been seen as symbolic of worry for at least 300 years, but to untie the knot before awaking was believed to lessen the problem considerably. It must never be cut, otherwise a separation from someone close was inevitable. To dream of tying a knot is said to presage meeting someone who will become a true friend. Modern dream research has, however, suggested that the knot also has a strong sexual conotation — carrying a warning about infidelity.

L

LABORATORY
Dreams of working in a laboratory can be traced back to the experiments of the alchemists in the Middle Ages and then, as now, such experiences are said to be a warning against expending too much energy in doubtful projects, when it could be better utilised in more practical matters. In more recent years the dream has come to be regarded as one of contrary and any imagined success in a laboratory is a pointer to failure — especially for men in their relationships with women. American sources believe that a dream of people working in a laboratory is advising caution in business dealings.

LABOUR
The builders of the mighty pyramids, the ancient Egyptians, were the first to report dreams of men at labour, and claimed the omens were good. To dream of others at work was said to indicate successful achievements and robust health! There is, however, no mention of dreams in which the sleeper imagines *himself* at work until the sixteenth century, and then such experiences were believed to signify a favourable outcome for any new enterprise. For farmers the dream pointed to a good harvest. The Victorians claimed that to dream of animals at work was a sign of prosperity but at the expense of any employees; while in

Europe to see labourers standing idle or in dispute fore-shadows an emotional upset for the dreamer.

LABYRINTH
Another of the famous obstacle dreams with the omens dependent on the outcome of the dream. For centuries it has been said that to be lost in any kind of labyrinth signifies becoming entangled in personal problems, especially with a partner or lover. If the labyrinth was shrouded in darkness, or appeared to be seen at night, then the omens indicated a prolonged illness. Authorities are agreed that to find a way out of the labyrinth will minimise the problems, but the warning should not be ignored. In Europe, to dream of being lost in a labyrinth of roads foretells a tortuous journey; while several recent American almanacs feel that the dream is pointing to the end of a mystery that has been puzzling the dreamer.

LACE
For many centuries the Chinese have held lace to be an omen of fidelity in love, and in the West, too, to dream of any garments made from lace symbolises success with the opposite sex. Women who dream of lace will achieve current ambitions, say a number of European sources, though to dream of making and selling lace is a warning against over-reaching capabilities. French sources claim that a young girl who dreams of wearing lace underwear will find a handsome lover; while in America, the girl who dreams of being given lace by a lover is destined for a long life

LADDER
Jacob's famous dream in the Bible of seeing a ladder reaching up to Heaven indicates the antiquity of this type of experience. In general, to dream of climbing a ladder offers the chance to advance in all areas of personal and business life, though to fall from one points to some bad luck in financial matters or a personal relationship. Broken rungs

are a caution against being over-ambitious, but to feel dizzy while on a ladder is a sign of a very beneficial event about to occur. To dream of other people on a ladder signifies the dreamer has a number of good friends who can help in a current crisis, although to imagine using a ladder to enter any building is a warning against dubious ambitions. Curiously, British sources believe that a dream of walking under a ladder — so ill-omened in superstition — is actually a good luck sign!

LAKES

European sources claim that dreams of clear and placid lakes are a pointer to happiness and good relationships; while a turbulent or muddy lake is symbolic of upheavals and problems. Such dreams have been particularly prevalent among young woman, and a number of old almanacs claim that a moonlit lake augurs well for love-affairs. However, to dream of wading or swimming in a lake is a warning against promiscuity. In America, the bigger the lake the better the current love-affair, though one where the water is absolutely still is said to prophesy being jilted.

LAMBS

Lambs are as pleasing a sight in dreams as they are in real life, and for many centuries to imagine them grazing or playing has augured well for home life and general happiness. Rural almanacs claim that to dream of carrying a baby lamb means 'you will be encumbered with happy cares upon which you will lavish a wealth of devotion', though to see them distressed or being killed will be followed by a period of depression through failing to accept responsibilties. A curious Victorian book of dream lore warns against eating lamb chops, as this denotes illness and a lot of anxiety over children! On a more serious note, Australian authorities say that to dream of buying lambs points to a welcome surprise, while American sources believe that to dream of shearing lambs is a sure sign of prosperity.

LAMP

For close on 2,000 years the lamp has been symbolic in dream lore of achievement and prosperity, as a reward for hard work. Lighted oil lamps were first thought to indicate domestic bliss, and it was only flickering or broken ones that pointed to illness in the family. The omens have changed very little since the introduction of gas and then electric lamps, and just as dreaming of carrying a lantern was symbolic of self-confidence, so the light of a modern torch is an encouragement for the dreamer to follow his or her own convictions. In Europe, dreaming of a lamp will lead to an unexpected inheritance, while in the East dreams of many-coloured lamps point to an equally unexpected festivity. American sources add that to dream of switching on a lamp presages having to explain some awkward activities to others, while turning off a lamp prophesies the end of a love-affair.

LAND

The omens behind a dream of owning land depend upon the conditions of the land, according to the old almanacs. Obviously rich and fertile land augurs well for prosperity (in the case of young girls the likelihood of meeting a husband), while dry and barren acres point to failure and unhappiness. Since the last century, the dream has also been widely interpreted as a subconscious desire for a permanent home; though some sources state that to imagine owning land, when the dreamer is already the possessor of some, indicates that a change of occupation is imminent.

LAP

Several Victorian almanacs mention dreams of sitting in the lap of a member of the opposite sex, and the implications of this activity. One claims the dream signifies a 'pleasant security from vexing engagements', while another believes it to be a caution about an unsuitable admirer. Modern authorities accept the sexual implications of the dream, citing the earliest references from the Middle Ages, when young women were warned that a serpent in the lap foretold the ruination of their modesty; while a cat in the same position was a warning against the designs of a seducer. Today the dream is regarded as signifying a new love-affair, though if the person on the lap falls off, the dreamer is about to be ridiculed.

LATE

Dreams of being late, or being frustrated in getting somewhere on time, have been reported in a number of recent dream surveys, and the omens drawn from these experiences vary. In America, for example, the feeling is that the dreamer is about to have his or her opinions sought, while European sources favour the explanation that the subconscious is warning against making promises that cannot be kept. Both authorities, though, are agreed that to see other people being late presages a loss of money.

LAUGHTER

A generally ill-omened dream, especially if other people appear to be laughing at the dreamer. The first reported instances of this dream occurred approximately 400 years ago when visions of being laughed at by enemies were seen as indicating illness. A disembodied laugh was said to be a warning against indiscreet love-affairs, while a group of people laughing symbolised the dreamer becoming the object of gossip or losing a close friend. More recently, some European sources have stated this to be a dream of contrary, especially if the dreamer was laughing at others, for this indicated approaching unhappiness. However, authorities are unanimous that children seen laughing in a dream are a sign of a small financial windfall.

LAWYERS

Lawyers have featured widely in dreams for several

hundred years, and the omens accorded to them vary from the serious to the frivolous. Lawyers were first believed to be symbolic of worry and problems, and to dream of seeking their help was a warning to be on guard against malicious gossip. A century ago young ladies were advised that to dream of a lawyer indicated they would unwittingly commit indiscretions; while young men could expect money difficulties. Recent study, however, has shown that any dream of the law is a warning about carelessness in personal matters, and that to imagine winning a case actually points to losing a vital argument. To dream of being sued is also said by British sources to be a warning against casual love-affairs.

LAZY
It may be pleasant to dream of being lazy, but the omens recorded since the Middle Ages point to various problems thereafter. To dream of neglecting business or domestic matters, for example, will lead to disagreements in the family, while for a man or woman to feel his or her partner is lazy signifies the ill-will of a third party. A quaint Victorian source told its female readers that if a girl dreamed that her lover was lazy 'she will have bad luck in securing admiration, for her actions will discourage men who mean marriage'! An equally strange American almanac claims that to dream of children being lazy ensures they will marry wealthy people!

LEATHER
Dreams of leather items are symbolic of successful business deals and happy love-affairs. Some of the earliest records of this type of dream are to be found in French sources, where to be dressed from head to toe in leather presaged luck in any speculation. British authorities, too, state that ornaments of leather indicate faithfulness in love, while American almanacs claim that to dream of buying leather presages a happy time for the family.

LEAVES

Rural almanacs claim that leaves are particularly reliable omens in dreams, green leaves signifying good health; brown leaves poor health; falling leaves indicating the separation of friends; and leaves blowing in the wind pointing to family quarrels. A carpet of dead leaves through which the dreamer has to drag his or her feet presages loneliness, say European sources, while a young woman who dreams of plucking fresh young leaves from a tree will soon meet a vigorous lover. In America, green leaves are said to be symbolic of coming into money, while withered leaves which are seen still hanging on a tree indicate a death in the family. A recent British survey has also concluded that dreams of falling leaves are symptomatic of a life being wasted away, and that the sleeper should act more positively.

LEGS

The Greeks first instigated the various omens concerning dreams of legs; the most important was that to see a pair of legs (either the dreamer's or another person's) which were injured or deformed was symbolic of poverty. Thin legs were said to be a warning about a forthcoming embarrassing situation, while to dream of losing a leg would result in the loss of a relative. In Europe in the eighteenth century a married woman who dreamed of having beautiful legs was said to be about to go on a long journey; while if she dreamed of having hairy legs she would dominate her husband! Modern British sources claim that for a man or woman to dream of beautiful legs on a member of the opposite sex promises a very satisfying love-affair.

LENDING

The act of lending in a dream exercised the minds of numerous earlier authorities, who concluded it to be another instance of contrary where the dreamers would, in fact, soon be in need of some money themselves. Equally ill-omened is to lend clothes, which indicates troubles ahead, or to lend domestic items, which will result in family arguments. A Victorian source said that a dream of refusing to lend *anything* would nonetheless retain the respect of friends. A recent American book of dream lore adds that to imagine lending a car will lead to 'a change in environment'.

LETTERS
Dreams about letters predate the introduction of the postal service by many years, but the passage of time has done little to change the omens. To dream of receiving a letter indicates good news unless the contents prove to be disturbing which points to personal problems. Eighteenth-century almanacs declared that dreams about love-letters were good omens, promising a happy marriage; but modern sources suggest they are symbolic of a guilty secret, and that to imagine writing one is actually a sign of regret over a foolish love-affair. A registered letter promises a new job; an anonymous or torn letter is a warning about a rival in love; and an envelope with black on it presages a death. European sources claim that to imagine reading a letter addressed to someone else signifies a financial loss, while American authorities believe that any dream about a letter containing a demand for money is a warning to take care in all business dealings. A recent British survey has also advised that any dream about letters actually presages the arrival of some vital news — though probably not as bad as expected.

LEWDNESS
Lewd behaviour in dreams appears to be a particularly Western trait and almanacs, over the past two centuries, have agreed it to be a warning against becoming involved in nefarious activities. If the dreamer is being lewd, then the activity will probably be to do with business, while if it is

134

someone else behaving in this manner then the omen is concerned with sexual relationships.

LIGHTHOUSE
The lighthouse has become quite a feature of modern dreams, but it is the conditions in which it is seen that are crucial to the omens. The consensus of opinion is that a lighthouse amid a placid sea points to a period of contentment with congenial friends — probably on holiday — while a lighthouse battered by a storm, or being damaged, indicates an unsettling period of life, though of short duration. American sources state that to dream of going to a lighthouse will lead to success at work; while leaving one presages the arrival of an important letter. The best of these dreams, says a recent British source, is to imagine being *inside* a lighthouse: this augurs well for a long and happy life.

LION
The lion, the 'King of the animal world', has featured prominently in dream lore since biblical times when it was first seen as symbolising power and authority. Many nations believe the dream to be specially relevant to men, indicating they have the chance to succeed in business and social life; while for a young woman it means a new and fascinating lover. In Europe, a caged lion signifies the dreamer will have strong opposition to current plans, while to be chased by a lion presages some form of disgrace. To see young lions is a pointer to new friendships, while the death of a lion is believed to foreshadow the death of a prominent person. According to recently published research, the lion often appears in dreams of middle-age, symbolising the uncontrolled energy against which the dreamers have to measure themselves in the future.

LOCK
A legend, several centuries old, claims that a dream of

135

placing a lock upon a woman was the inspiration for the notorious chastity belt. True or not, locks have long been associated with sexual fidelity. Eastern sources claim that a man who dreams of opening a lock will have several lovers; while a woman will be unfaithful to her partner. A British authority says that to dream of picking a lock points to an embarrassment due to involvement in someone else's affairs, while the French claim that the sight of an opened lock indicates the moment is right to begin a new courtship.

LOCOMOTIVE
The locomotive is symbolic of travel and in some instances the possibility of unexpected visitors. European books of dream lore claim that to see a locomotive at speed indicates a rapid promotion, though for one to be involved in an accident points to the loss of some property. British sources believe there are good omens in driving a train — such as an inheritance — while in America, a vision of a locomotive disappearing into the distance points to the loss of a lover.

LOST
To dream of being lost is an experience of contrary, for it presages happiness in social life. To lose someone in a dream is also a good omen for it indicates being reunited with an old friend. In Europe, to dream of becoming lost with a friend means the arrival of some welcome news, while the Americans believe that to lose a piece of property, such as a car, points to a financial windfall. It is, though, bad luck to dream of losing a child for this presages domestic troubles.

LOVE
Dreams of love are truly universal and point to happiness and contentment. The first records indicated that love of parents was symbolic of prosperity and good fortune; love between husband and wife represented security and fidelity; and to love children indicated happiness and longevity.

In the Middle Ages, a dream of being unloved was said to warn of sickness, while the person who visualised being loved by many people was a prey to vanity. The Victorians claimed that to love work promised prosperity, and, curiously, the man or woman who dreamed of not being loved would eventually marry and live happily. An American source has also recently suggested that to dream of being loved by relatives indicates financial losses!

LUGGAGE
Luggage is believed to symbolise travel, though some authorities suggest it can equally relate to being encumbered by people. For instance, in Europe, dreams of baggage indicate a trip abroad, though in America to visualise being surrounded by a pile of luggage is a warning of being pestered by people for money. To lose luggage points to family arguments unless the dream occurs to an engaged person, when the implication is that the proposed marriage is under threat. Recent study has also argued that the dream may well be symbolic of a secret the dreamer is concealing, but would be wiser confessing.

LYING
Authorities are divided on the omens of dreams about lying. Some early almanacs claimed the dreamer who imagined lying to escape punishment would implicate an innocent person, while other sources believed the person who lied to protect his friends would suffer terrible criticism. European authorities now feel that to dream of telling lies will lead to trouble, because the sleeper has been behaving foolishly, while several American sources claim it is symbolic of a long and happy life. To dream of other people lying is, however, accepted on both sides of the Atlantic as an indication of unexpected help to solve a difficult problem.

M

MACHINERY

Machinery has been a part of dream lore since the Industrial Revolution, one of the earliest omens on record declaring that a vision of machinery powered by steam 'fortells of happiness and prosperity'. Good omens have continued to be associated with machinery ever since. European sources, for example, declaring it to be indicative of starting new ventures which, while not easy, will eventually come to fruition. Smooth-running machinery is said in Britain to symbolise success in current efforts; while inefficient or broken machinery will cause set-backs to ambition. In America, to feel afraid of machinery is a warning to be cautious about new plans.

MAGIC

Dreams of making magic can be found in documents from the time of the Roman Empire, when they were said to symbolise changes in life. To dream of being a magician indicates a pleasant surprise is imminent; while to watch someone else performing magical tricks indicates some interesting journeys lie ahead. British sources claim that to dream of being mystified by magic will lead to a reunion with a long-lost friend, or the reviving of an old love-affair; while in America, to imagine being present at a magic show presages some unexpected good news.

MAKE-UP

Women have been using make-up for centuries, and it is interesting to find that the earliest omens on record — in the sixteenth century — declare that for a man to dream of a lady 'making-up' her face was a warning that he was going to be deceived! A woman who had this dream was no better off, for she 'would have trouble in her love-affairs'. The omens about cosmetics do seem to have changed over the intervening years, for nowadays they are said to be a good omen for women, promising financial security and a satisfactory love-life. Men, too, can look for happy relationships with the opposite sex, if they dream of a woman applying her make-up.

MANACLES

This is a dream of contrary, for people who dream of wearing manacles or handcuffs can look forward to escaping the worries that have been plaguing them of late. This omen must have cheered the people of Europe in the fifteenth century, just as the suggestion that to see others in manacles ensured the dreamer's safety and protection from evil-doers. To see an enemy in manacles was, curiously, believed to be an omen of success in trade. Modern authorities continue to accept this symbolism, having added the definition that to dream of snapping a pair of handcuffs on someone else is going to lead to a dramatic improvement in the dreamer's lifestyle!

MAN

For a girl to dream of a handsome man she does not know has been considered for centuries as an omen of financial luck rather than an affair of the heart. An ugly man, on the other hand, portends trouble with someone thought to be a friend. Dream books of the seventeenth century warned girls who had a dream of a man carrying weapons that sickness was imminent; while young Victorian ladies were informed that a 'well-formed and supple man' foretold a

139

life 'vastly enjoyed with many rich possessions'. The omens concerning today's 'dream man' are believed to be governed by his appearance and surroundings. On the whole, the dream augurs more for social engagements and new friends than for a love-affair.

MANUSCRIPT
Many an author must have dreamed of manuscripts, and almanacs have been listing the omens associated with them for close on 300 years. To dream of an unfinished manuscript signifies it will never be published (according to several European sources); while an American authority states that any unfinished piece of writing points to disappointment in a current project — literary or not. A popular Victorian dream book informed its readers that to imagine burning a manuscript would ensure at least some of the dreamer's literary work would enjoy publication.

MAPS
For 2,000 years maps in dreams have symbolised travel and journeys, although the earliest omens pointed out that unless the land masses on the map were clearly defined, the trips would be fraught with danger. Later authorities claimed the larger the map, the farther the journey would be, and the more colourful it was the more rewarding the experience. American sources have recently claimed that to dream of consulting a map indicates a change of business or employment, while a German book says that a young woman doing this is looking for an exciting new lover. A dream survey has also suggested that the experience symbolises the exploitation of talent, and that dreamers would be well advised to ensure that they have worked out their real objectives in life.

MARCHING
The ancient Romans used to tell their sons that a dream of marching was an omen indicating they would become

soldiers. By the seventeenth century, however, the dream was said to presage bad news, and that the longer the dreamer imagined tramping the countryside the more likely the news would indicate a death in the family. Victorian almanacs informed female readers that to dream of marching men was a sign they aspired to marry a man in a public position; but if they imagined themselves alongside the marchers, they were in danger of losing their honour. Modern sources have claimed that a dream of marching indicates a need to seek the help of others for a project that would be best served by teamwork.

MARKET
Rural almanacs have, naturally, claimed any dream of a market is a good omen signifying prosperity, as long, of course, as the market is flourishing and the stalls are well-stocked. A deserted market with decaying produce was a sign of ill-health, and for a woman to dream of an empty stall in a market-place was said to indicate she would soon have an empty cot in her home. Modern sources have stated that to dream of being in a busy public market is a sign of new friendships, though to be idling time away there is a warning about missing opportunities.

MASK
Masks have apparently featured in dreams for many centuries, although most of the omens have originated from comparatively recent European sources. The consensus of opinion is that the mask symbolises deceit, and the dreamer is being warned about being tricked by a rival in business or love. Italian authorities believe that the dreamer who imagines wearing a mask will have a problem with a member of the family as the result of a misunderstanding; while a Spanish source has suggested it means making a lot of money! An interesting recent British almanac says that those who dream of wearing a mask will end up by benefiting from a scheme intended to cheat them.

MEAL

Eating a meal is generally considered as a dream of contrary: the more lavish the dishes, the harder the problems the dreamer will be facing. The idea that a frugal meal is symbolic of prosperity and plenty appears to date from the early years of Christianity, although authorities are agreed that meat dishes are indicative of happiness — except when the meat is raw, which presages the death of a friend. A recent explanation from a British authority says that any dream about a meal signifies that an interruption will shortly take place to an important event or a business engagement. Throwing any remains of a meal away during a dream is a warning against extravagance.

MEDALS

While European sources believe any dream in which medals feature signifies recognition for worthwhile achievements, in America the dream is read more simply as signifying the successful ending of a time of anxiety. To see other people with medals, according to British authorities, is a warning to control jealous impulses; while to lose a medal points to some bad luck in business through the carelessness of others. A girl who dreams of medals is in for an exciting period of social activity.

MEDICINE

The earliest dreams of medicine were read as straightforward omens of sickness, though several nineteenth-century authorities reversed this definition by claiming it to be a dream of contrary. If, they said, the dreamer imagined taking the medicine himself, then he would enjoy good health, but should he imagine administering it to another person, this signified causing pain to a trusting friend. Following research in the last 20 years, a British authority has claimed that the dream is symbolic of the need for a medical check-up before a serious illness develops.

MENDING

Mending and sewing clothes are familiar dream experiences according to the old almanacs, which define them as being signs not of hard work, but of financial gain. Repairing soiled and dirty garments comes in for mention in several seventeenth-century documents, which state that the dreamer is about to be engaged in righting a wrong. European sources agree that to see other people mending clothes is a warning to be cautious in love-affairs; while a recent Italian almanac says that the young girl who dreams of mending garments will prove a great support to her future husband.

MICE

Mice have long featured in dream lore, where they are said to symbolise domestic problems for a woman and business worries for a man. A lone mouse in a dream has also been described as a warning to be careful about the activities of an acquaintance. The Victorians believed that to see a cat killing a mouse signified an end to a current problem; if the mouse escaped then the problems would be redoubled. The French claim that a woman who dreams of a mouse on her clothing is destined to be the subject of a scandal.

MILK

Milk is symbolic of good health, and rural almanacs claim the farmer who dreams of drinking a glass can be sure of a good harvest. The Romans believed that to dream of bathing in milk signified happiness and pleasant companions; and in real life, the wealthier members of society actually practised this. From the Middle Ages, a dream of spilt milk indicated a loss of business; hot milk pointed to a family argument; and sour milk would lead to the loss of a friend. More recent European sources state that a married woman who dreams of jugs of milk will soon be pregnant; while a man will go on a long and successful business trip.

MINING

European sources for the past 300 years have claimed that to dream of a mine indicated that the dreamer would eventually come into some money through his or her own efforts. Dreams of being a miner, however, are not quite so propitious. To imagine going down into a mine is a caution to trust only close friends in any current project; while to emerge from a mine is a sign of an unfaithful wife. In America, to dream of owning a gold mine is a warning to the dreamer that he or she is going to be guilty of some foolish actions.

MIRROR

The ancient Egyptians first declared that it was a bad omen to dream of seeing one's face in a mirror, because this signified the death of the dreamer or a member of the family — no doubt an echo of the myth of Narcissus who drowned while staring at his own reflection in water. The passage of time has changed this omen, however; in the Far East, for instance, the dreamer who sees a member of his or her family in a mirror will become wealthy, while in Europe the dreamer is in danger of being robbed. All authorities are agreed that to dream of a broken mirror presages bad news and sadness. Modern research has also stated that to see the faces of other people in a mirror is a caution to watch out for being dishonestly treated.

MONEY

Another dream topic which has caused great differences of opinion ever since coins were introduced. The consensus of opinion is that the omens are better if the dreamer was giving *or* lending money, thus signifying prosperity; receiving money indicates security *only* if it was honestly come by. The early authorities agreed that to dream of finding money signified small business worries, while to steal it presaged a long illness. An interesting German source claimed that to dream of swallowing money pointed to the sleeper becoming mercenary. Several modern books of dream lore maintain that to dream of spending money will produce an unexpected profit, while to lose some will result in a surprise cheque in the post!

MONKEY

Perhaps a little unkindly, the monkey has been described as symbolic of deceit, and to see one in a dream is a warning against being deceived by people endeavouring to promote their own interests. A French source says that a woman who dreams of feeding a monkey will be seduced by flattery; while an American authority maintains that to see monkeys in a cage means disappointment in love-affairs. A British book of dream lore published 50 years ago adds, curiously, that a young woman who dreams of a monkey 'should insist on an early marriage as her lover will suspect unfaithfulness'.

MOON

According to ancient Egyptian sources, to dream of the moon was considered favourable and signified pardon, though by Roman times it was believed to present a feminine, even maternal, aspect. Since Roman times, though, a number of different dreams about the moon have been associated with love. A full moon, for instance, is said to be symbolic of a vigorous sex life; while a man who dreams of being bathed in moonlight will soon have a new lover. In the Middle Ages, a dream of a blood-red moon signified strife, while a moon partly covered by clouds pointed to family problems. A new moon is said to be good for business affairs, and rural almanacs have stated that a harvest moon foretells financial benefits. Recent studies have also revealed that moonlight reflected on water in a dream is an omen of good luck for a young woman, indicating a new man in her life.

145

MOTHER

Another dream noted since antiquity, and one with the most favourable omens. To dream of talking to, or embracing, a mother is symbolic of very good news, and should she be in the family home then success in business ventures is promised. European authorities have said that if the mother is in blooming health, then a family reunion is imminent. Any indication of sickness happily does not relate to her, but is a warning about the dreamer's lifestyle. A recent British source believes that a dream of a mother being dead is a warning of a personal danger to the sleeper.

MOTOR CAR

Obviously such dreams are of recent origin, and the general opinion is that the car signifies a forthcoming piece of news: if it is speeding, then the news will be imminent, and vice versa. A car that refuses to start is indicating that a change in objectives would be advisable; while to dream of driving a new car signifies that a change of job will soon occur. A European source believes that to visualise driving a car at night means the dreamer is hiding a guilty secret; while a recent American book of dream lore claims that to be in an automobile accident is another case of contrary — very soon the sleeper is going to come into some money!

MOUNTAIN

Climbing mountains while asleep is another of the classic obstacle dreams. To reach the top is symbolic of success in life, but to fail on the slopes points to obstacles in either family or business matters. In the mountainous regions of Europe, a girl who dreams of climbing with a male companion is said to be in danger of seduction; while in parts of Asia a vision of a mountain is said to signify a difficult delivery for any relative or friend of the dreamer who is pregnant. A recent Italian almanac has also claimed that to awaken while in a perilous position on a mountainside actually presages a success in life when failure seemed more likely! A British source has also suggested that mountains may symbolise an element of stability as well as a challenge to energy and action.

MOVIES
Watching a film is another recent dream omen, and the consensus of opinion says that a movie which the dreamer enjoyed points to an invitation to a happy social occasion. If the picture was upsetting in any way, then beware of taking foolish actions. A British source claims that if members of the family are present at the movie then a period of domestic happiness will follow; while a recent American almanac has stated that to dream of appearing in a film is symbolic of a change in lifestyle.

MOVING
Moving from a house (or nowadays including an apartment) has featured in dream lore for a good many years, although it does not necessarily presage an actual move, but rather the overcoming of some problems in life. In other words, if the move goes smoothly, then a number of difficulties will be removed, but an incomplete move suggests that a reappraisal would be advisable. A European source has stated that if other people are moving (in the dream) then some friends are planning a surprise; while in America a dream of successfully moving from one house to another foretells the recovery of some missing valuable items.

MURDER
To dream of murder is not only unpleasant but also ill-omened. The ancient Greeks first believed this to be a prophecy of sorrow and failure; later writers declared that if the dreamer was the killer it signified he would shortly be disgraced because of his involvement in some dishonest adventure. To suffer the threat of murder, according to several European sources, is a warning of underhand dealings by rivals. An American book of dream lore recently

suggested that to see other people committing a murder was a sign of a long life.

MUD
Dream lore contains innumerable references to the sensation of sinking into mud, or the appearance of formless muddy characters. Because it is a product of earth and water, it is therefore seen as symbolising creation. The earliest sources claimed any dream about mud foretold coming into some hidden riches — probably gold; while sinking into mud would lead to a rapid recovery from illness, because of the healing powers of the mixture. For the past 200 years or so, to imagine being enveloped by mud has been interpreted as forecasting a scandal; while moulding or shaping mud would bring about good luck. Freud has stated that dreams of mud reveal an anal fixation, although others have argued that mud cannot be equated with excrement as it is not a by-product of the human body.

MUSICAL INSTRUMENTS
Italian and German sources provide some of the earliest omens concerning dreams of playing musical instruments. Their opinions suggest that this activity presages some new-found pleasures in life, and it matters not whether the dreamer can actually play the instrument in question. To dream of a broken instrument predicts the end of a friendship, although to visualise repairing the instrument will bring good news — probably in relation to a love-affair. A British source has also reported that to dream of carrying a musical instrument is 'a sign of success with the opposite sex'.

MYSTERY
To have the sensation of being involved in some kind of mystery has attracted the attention of writers on dream lore since the Middle Ages. The earliest definition suggests the dreamer is going to be harassed by strangers in need of his

or her help, although several European sources believe it may be a warning not to neglect duties to which the sleeper has an aversion. Writing recently, a British authority has gone farther and claimed that any dream of mystery is symbolic of being enveloped in self-induced worries, something which simple relaxation techniques could soon relieve.

N

NAKED
Another of the famous experiences in dream lore often stated to symbolise openness and vulnerability. It was seemingly not long after men and woman had started to clothe themselves that dreams of running naked like their forebears began to intrude into the sleeping hours. The Romans first declared the dream to be an omen of unhappiness and even scandal, though within a couple of centuries the girl who dreamed of herself naked was stated to be arrogant; while a man was worrying over the revelation of some secret. After the Middle Ages, a girl who dreamed of disporting herself in the nude was seeking an illicit affair, and a man had apparently lost his ambition. In today's world, the dreamer who appears without trousers or a dress will enjoy a little financial luck; although to see strangers going naked is a warning of being unduly trusting of others. An American source has further suggested that to dream of nudity is symbolic of a fear of being the subject of gossip, or having some secret 'exposed'.

NAMES
Names have a special significance, primarily because of the frequency with which they are mentioned in dreams quoted in the Bible. From these origins has come the belief that to dream of hearing your own name signifies good news,

though to be called by the wrong name indicates personal problems ahead. For several centuries to dream of calling a loved one's name has been said to result in a happy reunion with that person; while to call a child's name will bring that youngster good fortune. A recent British source has added that to dream of being unable to remember your own name is a warning against an illicit affair.

NARROW

The sensation of being in somewhere narrow — a street, a mountain pass, or hemmed in by undergrowth — is now accepted as a rather unwelcome obstacle dream. European sources have seen it as symbolising a hard struggle for the dreamer to achieve any kind of business or personal success; but if other people are met in the narrow divide, then success is possible with great effort. An American authority recently concluded that the dream could indicate being too ambitious in certain objectives, and that it would be a good idea to seek some help.

NAVEL

Buddhists have for centuries claimed that a dream of Buddha contemplating his navel is an omen of good fortune, and this definition has been adopted by other cultures to indicate that any dream in which a navel features signifies a new project is about to materialise. In Europe, it is said that to dream of another person's navel signifies the beginning of a new love-affair.

NAVY

Nautical almanacs claim that a dream of the navy is symbolic of an inner struggle to combat difficulties, as well as a yearning for faraway places. In the great maritime nations, such dreams were said to come true unless the dreamer was frightened at the prospect of going to sea, or the navy vessels appeared unseaworthy. A European source claims that to dream of seeing friends in the navy presages sickness; while an American almanac has stated that a married man who dreams of serving in the navy is apparently being given an inkling that his wife is committing adultery.

NECKLACE

Interestingly, while any dream featuring a neck is said to prophesy a financial benefit, a necklace is symbolic of love and happiness. Roman sources believed that people of either sex who visualised themselves wearing a necklace would enjoy positions of honour and wealth. By the sixteenth century, to dream of receiving a necklace was said to presage a long life, and a man who dreamed of giving one to his sweetheart would make her his slave. To lose a necklace, or have it break, however, will be followed by a family quarrel or lover's tiff, according to European sources.

NEEDLE

The omens about needles are mixed, although one of the earliest accounts of this dream states that it is a symbol of intrigue! European records dating from the fourteenth century claimed that to be pricked by a needle presaged family difficulties brought about by the bad luck of a relative. To lose a needle was a warning of danger occurring as a result of the dreamer's carelessness. To thread a needle, however, is a lucky omen, expecially in matters of love as it will bind the dreamer closer to her partner. An American source has suggested that to find a needle will result in an appreciative new friend. Those who dream of seeing a needle being pointed at them are getting a warning that someone is being spiteful about them behind their backs.

NEIGHBOURS

To dream of talking and laughing cheerfully with neighbours is a dream of contrary for it presages problems with these same people. An American authority has written that to imagine meeting a neighbour on the street will result in an unwelcome guest, while to go visiting neighbours can cause a family row. Some European sources, however, disagree with this definition and claim that a dream of helping a neighbour will result in a small financial benefit.

NETS

Omens associated with nets probably originated in the ancient world, and there are quite distinct definitions for dreams about using them or becoming entangled. Fishermen first believed that to imagine using a net promised success in their occupation, although actually to see fish in the net was a bad omen, because it presaged stormy weather which could well prevent them putting to sea. Indeed, by the Middle Ages a dream of ensnaring anything in a net indicated the dreamer would be unscrupulous in his dealings. In more recent times, a woman who dreams of using a net can look forward to a long and happy marriage; while a man will soon fall in love. The sensation of being entangled in a net is believed to signify that the dreamers have troubles which they feel they cannot escape, and they should seek advice.

NEWSPAPERS

Although newspapers have featured in dreams for less than 200 years, they are still believed to be significant symbols. European sources say they indicate travel; American authorities suggest that a death is imminent; and in Britain that events are conspiring in the dreamer's favour. The French claim that to see a member of the opposite sex buying a newspaper presages a love-affair. A Canadian almanac reported recently that a dream of other people reading newspapers is a warning about becoming the subject of gossip. If it is possible to read the name of anyone in the newspaper — including the dreamer's own — then that person will enjoy a little fame.

NIGHTMARE

A nightmare from which the dreamer awakes screaming and shaking can be the result of undergoing quite a few of the experiences listed in this book. But to dream of having an actual nightmare is a comparatively rare occurrence, though it has been listed in almanacs for several centuries. Earlier authorities claimed that it prophesied failure and disappointment, but perhaps most importantly a need to watch matters of health. Modern sources believe a nightmare represents deep-seated emotional problems which are being repressed, and advise seeking psychological help. To imagine walking at night, in a state of fear, has also been listed with the nightmare as an omen of troubles ahead.

NIPPLE

The ancient Greeks first recorded the dream of seeing a person with three nipples, and believed this to be a sign that the sleeper has an inordinately strong sex drive. Later authorities have agreed that any dream about nipples is related to sex, and that the larger and more appealingly coloured they are the better the omens of compatibility and success with the opposite sex. To dream of a child suckling at its mother's breasts is believed to signify an end to current worries — according to most European sources — though one authority does suggest it can also mean an improvement in finances.

NOSE

Roman lore had a particular fascination with noses, believing strongly that a dream of a bleeding nose was symbolic of disaster. They also felt that to dream of a beautiful nose was a boost to self-confidence, though a nose that looked smaller than usual pointed to a series of failures. More recent authorities have suggested the bleeding nose is symbolic of financial problems; while a big nose indicates sexual prowess! A curved nose on a woman is said to signify

154

adultery (according to American sources), while a British authority has written that a dream of having a blocked or damaged nose is a warning about opposition to the dreamer's wishes.

NUMBERS
Though it is not unusual to have a dream in which numbers occur, it is rare for the dreamer to remember them on waking. For this reason, authorities have tended to generalise the omens: a Victorian almanac declaring, for instance, that the dream 'denotes unsettled conditions in business, which will cause you unease and dissatisfaction', while a recent American book claimed that counting numbers 'will result in good news'. A modern British source believes the dream is actually symbolic of a period of confusion and surprises. A European writer has suggested that if the dreamer can remember a number from the dream it is a lucky omen and should be employed in a little bit of gambling!

NURSE
The nurse is universally regarded in dreams as a good omen, especially if she is seen in a hospital situation, as this indicates good health. The Victorians had reservations about a nurse entering a house, as they felt this was a sign of forthcoming illness, though American sources are inclined to the view that monetary problems are more likely. British writers claim that a single person who dreams of a nurse is in line for getting married; while for a married person, family unity is promised. A European almanac has also claimed that any young girl who dreams of needing the help of a nurse has unwittingly become pregnant.

NUTS
Dreams about nuts have been recorded for several centuries as good omens. From the seventeenth century, to gather nuts in a dream was said to signify a new love-affair;

while to crack nuts pointed to success in business. The person who dreamed of collecting nuts stood a chance of coming into some money, said European sources, though if the nuts were in poor condition then problems were brewing because of deceit. Eating nuts has always been seen as an omen of good health.

O

OAK TREES

The first dream omens concerning oaks are to be found in medieval English documents where the tree is said to symbolise prosperity and longevity. Oak trees were, of course, sacred to the Druids, and for centuries the old almanacs declared that dreams about them would reveal mystic wisdom to the dreamer. More recently, European sources have said that a dream of oak trees laden with acorns indicates an inheritance; falling oak leaves signify a loss of love; and a dead or fallen oak tree presages the death of a close friend. A British authority also wrote recently that a dream of oak utilised in furniture, doors, or beams symbolises emotional security.

OAR

The ancient peoples knew all about dreams featuring oars, which they regarded as omens of warning. To imagine using an oar was said to foretell exhausting work on behalf of others; to break an oar would lead to family problems; while to lose one would frustrate current plans. Some European sources believe that to dream of rowing a small boat is actually a more promising omen, and the dreamer can expect to carry out some good business transactions. According to a recent American almanac, though, the oar is actually a symbol of frivolity.

OASIS

Some strange omens have been reported about oases, though in the Arab world dreams about these welcome sights have naturally enough always been regarded as symbolic of making a successful desert crossing. In Europe, to dream of an oasis presages finding a new friend; in Britain, success in an important new endeavour; and in America, to imagine discovering an oasis in the company of a group of other people points to some unhappy times in love-affairs!

OATS

Rural almanacs believe oats to be good omens, and farmers who dreamed about them could be sure of a plentiful harvest. For other people, oats portend financial gain. Since the Middle Ages, dreams of green oats have symbolised hard work, though with eventual success. Decayed oats, however, point to a period of impoverishment for the dreamer's family. Oatmeal is also regarded as a sign of good times coming, especially for the young girl who dreams of cooking it, for she will soon find a partner for life.

OBELISK

The earliest references to dreams of obelisks occur in the sixteenth century when one almanac writer claimed, 'An obelisk looming up stately and cold in your dreams is the forerunner of melancholy tidings.' Several Victorian sources, however, believed this four-sided pillar to be symbolic of wealth and an ability to make shrewd purchases in business. Nonetheless, modern dream researchers are even more convinced the obelisk is actually a phallic symbol, and it signifies doubts concerning sexual potency, which they believe could well be removed by better care of health.

OBITUARY

The omens concerning obituaries are another case of contrary: they are actually symbolic of good news.

Ecclesiastical records from the sixteenth century indicate that, even then, a dream of receiving the obituary notice of a relative or friend should be taken as a sign of good news, and if the obituary happened to be of an enemy then a happy event such as a wedding or a birth was forecast. Several European sources have recently added that a dream of having to write an obituary will probably result in some unpleasant duties; though during the course of these, a most attractive member of the opposite sex will be encountered.

OCCULT
Dreams of the occult are of uncertain age, though in the Middle Ages anyone who had a vision of a person with occult powers was said to be coming into secret knowledge that they would be able to use to their advantage. The occultists themselves tended to wrap their abilities in mystery and for this reason most seventeenth and eighteenth-century almanacs were inclined to define a dream of the occult as rather ill-omened, with a possible threat to sanity. Modern authorities, however, think the dream is symbolic of desiring a higher plane of consciousness.

OCEAN
Oceans have been a part of dream lore for many centuries and authorities are agreed that it is the state of the water that is crucial to the omen. A calm ocean is a good omen for travel; a stormy one is bad for the dreamer's ambitions, as he or she will have to show real determination to succeed. To travel over an ocean is a good sign for business deals, but if the ship founders or sinks this will have a bad effect on love-affairs. A British source says that to see ocean waves crashing onto the shore signifies quarrels at home. An American authority has recently gone against the accepted belief concerning calm oceans, by stating that what they really foretell is a stormy married life.

OFFICE

Although the Victorians believed that dreams about the office pertained to their business lives, modern sources think the omens relate more directly to personal matters. Nineteenth-century almanacs, for instance, stated that a dream of having an office signified prosperity as long as business was conducted honestly; while to see an office full of people foretold a promotion. Recent European authorities, however, claim that to dream of being in a new office predicts a change in the dreamer's love-life, and to have business worries is actually a pointer to arguments at home. A British almanac has also stated that to have a recurring dream of office life signifies the dreamer is becoming obsessed with work and should relax before it adversely affects his or her health.

OIL

It is perhaps no surprise to learn that a dream about oil foretells making a fortune; though only a century ago, at the height of the British Empire, this same dream was said to indicate a period of 'pleasurable enterprises'! The ancient Egyptians used to believe that a dream of being anointed by oil would make a man or woman influential in important matters of state; while a document from the Middle Ages reveals that the man who dreamed of dealing in oil, would be unsuccessful in lovemaking! Nowadays, to dream of spilling any oil presages a loss of business, although to find it on clothing indicates a small financial windfall. To dream of striking an oil well, an American source adds, is a sign that the dreamer has a trait of genius not yet realised!

ONIONS

The onion as a dream symbol can be traced back before the Middle Ages, although the interpretations vary. The earliest sources equate the vegetable with sorrow because of its ability to make the eyes water, and this appears to have been the case well into the nineteenth century, when one almanac said that to see a quantity of onions 'represents the amount of spite and envy that you will meet by being successful'. European authorities later claimed that eating onions would enable the dreamer to overcome all opposition, though in America they are said to signify an increase in wealth. A recent dream survey reported that the onion indicates a period of instability, and to peel one is a sign that a trusted friend has no depth, especially if after peeling off the layers the centre is hollow.

OPERA
Seventeenth century Italian sources are the earliest to list dreams about the opera, one document from Florence (where the first operas were staged) stating that to imagine attending a performance was symbolic of good friendships and successful business dealings. Later European sources, however, have claimed that the opera is actually symbolic of disorder in the family, while an American source says it is a warning about deceiving other people. A recent survey has added that the type of opera seen — be it dramatic, tragic or comic — is also indicative of what the future holds for the dreamer.

OPERATION
Dreams of undergoing an operation have been reported in a number of recent surveys, and the consensus of opinion is that the omens relate to everyday life rather than health. To be present while surgery is taking place, either as a patient or a witness, is a general caution about business dealings and new friendships, according to American sources; while in Britain the signs are that the dreamer will undergo a change in his or her lifestyle coupled with some unexpected news.

ORANGES
Although the orange was the golden apple from the Garden of the Hesperides, for at least 1,500 years

authorities have been divided as to the omens associated with the delicious fruit. Early writers thought they were a dream of contrary: that an orange tree signified the shedding of tears and that to peel an orange would result in the death of a relative. In the eighteenth century, to eat an orange was regarded as a bad omen, with sickness for family members being one forecast, and the end of a love-affair being the consequence for young women. Recent sources have suggested that drinking orange juice indicates a short but passionate love-affair; while a dream of orange blossom forecasts a wedding.

ORCHARD
One of the earliest omens associated with orchards stated, curiously, that to dream of seeing wild animals eating fallen fruit indicated the dreamer would lose some property 'in trying to claim what are not really your own belongings'! For centuries, though, orchards have been regarded as symbolising good fortune, and that to see one full of ripening fruit presages success in ambitions. European sources believe orchards full of green fruit point to slow progress in current plans; while an American almanac says they signify having some bad friends.

ORDERS
The Romans first reported dreams of giving or taking orders. If the dreamer was obeying them, then he or she could expect an improvement in life, though to be giving them pointed towards unhappiness in the family; especially if the dreamer was involved with the military in any way. Medieval sources suggested that to have orders disobeyed would lead to arguments with influential friends; while later European authorities reported that a dream of obeying orders would lead to a bigger family — regardless of whether the sleeper was a man or woman! Today, such dreams are generally held to be symbolic of a need to be more positive in making decisions.

ORGY

History suggests that the infamous Roman orgies inspired dreams of debauchery, which have been noted by almanacs and dream surveys for many years. A Victorian book of dream lore claimed that for a man to imagine participating in orgies was symbolic of the fear of catching syphilis through his promiscuity; while for a young girl it meant she was worried about being frigid. Modern research has put aside both ideas by stating that the dream is actually a warning to the sleeper that his or her excesses or repressions may well lead to trouble unless tempered by moderation.

ORPHAN

To dream of being an orphan haunted many Victorian children who believed the omens to be bad, although authorities had written for several centuries that the dream was symbolic of care and concern for others. To dream of helping orphans presaged new responsibilities, but to be in an orphanage indicated a change of surroundings. An American book of dream lore published between the two world wars claimed that to dream of an orphan would result in receiving some money from a stranger. Modern research believes the dream to be a warning of being unduly self-centred, as this will alienate valued friends.

OWL

The owl has featured in dream lore since the first records were kept and has consistently been seen as a bad omen, symbolising the approach of death. In the Middle Ages, to see or hear the unearthly sound of an owl in a dream presaged sorrow and unhappiness, though to kill the bird promised a relief from anxiety. Later almanacs thought the bird signified bad news of an absent relative or friend; while to hear the screech of an owl was a warning to be on guard against a deceitful friend. Today the owl still remains a

dream omen of disappointment, unless it flies away or is
driven off before the sleeper awakes.

OYSTER
One of the most famous dream stories concerns the author
Bram Stoker who is said to have dreamt the idea for his
exotic vampire novel, *Dracula*, after eating a plate of oysters! These tasty shellfish have, in fact, been considered
symbolic of sexual prowess and desires for many years. To
dream of eating them signifies a desire for sensual
pleasures, according to an eighteenth-century source. A
European authority later confirmed this by saying that to
imagine opening oysters represented a desire for seduction
regardless of the consequences. Recent surveys have rather
diluted these views: a British writer claims that to eat oysters is merely a sign of good luck in love-affairs; while the
same can be achieved in America by simply dreaming of
buying some!

P

PADDOCK

Many a rider must have dreamed of being in a paddock with some horses, and the omens for happiness are good. To dream of grooming horses foretells a lucky speculation, according to a British source; although an American dream writer has claimed that to imagine being in the paddock of a racecourse is a warning against any form of gambling. For a young girl to dream of leading horses around a paddock indicates she will soon have a man to lavish her love on, as well as the horses.

PAINTING

To dream of a house being painted is symbolic of plans coming to fruition, although since the days of the Victorians, to imagine having paint on the clothes is a warning of being made unhappy by the unjustified criticism of others. In Europe, to see a painter going up a ladder is said to indicate news of some important event; though if the man comes down, a love-affair is about to end. To dream of being a painter is believed, in America, to signify that the sleeper is actually very happy with the job he or she already has. In Britain it indicates that the subject is trying to hide a secret possession. A recent Australian almanac believes that any dream of painting is a suggestion that the dreamer

should be content with life as it stands, rather than forever
wanting something new.

PALACE
Sumptuous palaces have featured in the dreams of rich and
poor alike since the Middle Ages, and the consensus of
opinion is that they symbolise a general improvement in
the dreamer's prospects. The person who visualised lords
and ladies dancing in a palace was said to be promised new
friends, according to a seventeenth-century source;
although to wander the rooms and corridors of a large
palace, without meeting anyone, was a sign to be on the
look-out for enemies. In the eighteenth century, a young
woman who dreamed of a palace could expect to marry a
wealthy and important man. A recent British authority has
claimed that the dream is a warning against undue vanity
which, if not checked, will exasperate relatives and friends.

PALM TREES
The dream of palm trees and tropical islands is typical of a
number of sleep experiences, which symbolise a desire for
change and new experiences. Several Victorian almanacs
agreed that the young girl who imagined walking down an
avenue of palm trees could look forward to a faithful husband and a good home. In France, the palm tree is believed
to signify a new and higher position in life. A recent British
writer, however, believes it to be an omen of disappointment, which will probably be brought about by being let
down by a friend.

PANTHER
Indian dream lore describes the panther as an omen of evil
unless the sleeper kills it; although in South America it is
considered to be a symbol of victory over enemies. Several
eighteenth-century Western sources were agreed that to
dream of being frightened by a panther was a sign of a
business contract or love-match being unexpectedly

broken. In the United States, however, a recent dream almanac claims that to see a group of panthers indicates the dreamer will soon travel abroad. To imagine being attacked by one of the animals presages a success in personal matters.

PARACHUTE
Dreams of falling wearing a parachute have been reported several times in recent surveys and most authorities are inclined to associate the sensation with that of falling [see entry under this heading]. An Australian writer has claimed the dream is a warning against going to extremes; while a British counterpart believes it is a suggestion that without more effort the dreamer's ambitions will crash to the ground. In Europe, to glide down safely on a parachute is said to indicate a happy love-life, but a difficult descent points to being let down by someone who used to be relied upon. An interesting American source recently suggested that a dream of seeing a group of people parachuting presaged an increase in the family.

PARALYSIS
The sensation of being paralysed in a dream has been reported for the last two centuries, and although initially believed to be symbolic of dishonour, it is now thought to have connotations with sex. The Victorians thought the dream indicated financial problems; and for lovers, an end to their courtship. Recent research has concluded that the dream signifies sexual inhibition, and the greater the feeling of paralysis the bigger the worry about impotence in the case of a man, and frigidity in the case of a woman. An American study has also suggested that a feeling of being totally paralysed means that the dreamer is battling with his or her conscience over a matter of morality concerning someone of the opposite sex.

PARCEL

A dream of receiving a parcel or package predates the introduction of the postal service, and was first thought to indicate the return of an absent relative or friend. In the early part of this century, the definition was revised to indicate an imminent change of circumstances, though to drop the parcel pointed to having to carry out an unpleasant task. American sources now believe any dream featuring a package hints at receiving a gift of money, although European authorities think it is actually a warning about a person, or persons, who are going to start loading their troubles onto the dreamer.

PARK

Dreams of parklands can be traced back to the seventeenth century, when a well-kept park was believed to indicate a period of contentment and leisure. In Europe, to dream of being accompanied in a park by a lover signified a happy marriage, while American authorities share a widespread view that an untidy park signifies a period of loneliness and adjustment in the life of the dreamer. A recent British source has seen a deeper meaning in the dream, in that it signifies a need to relax and enjoy nature instead of relentlessly pursuing mercenary objectives.

PARROT

The parrot is believed to be symbolic of gossip, according to most dream authorities. European sources claim that dreams of the bird can also point to becoming frivolous and running the danger of being the subject of ridicule. A chattering parrot points to business problems, according to a British source; while a dead bird foretells the departure of some friends. A charming French almanac published recently claims that a young woman who dreams of owning a parrot will be considered quarrelsome by her lover. An American source suggests just as amusingly of this same experience that on waking the dreamer should 'inquire about her fiancé's family'!

PARTY
Dreams of parties are generally considered ill-omened, which may well be a throw-back to the tradition in the Middle Ages that those who dreamed of finding themself amongst a party of carousing men would soon afterwards be robbed. Nowadays, according to European sources, to give a party presages quarrels; to dream of being given one will lead to a disappointment in love; while if the party becomes noisy and out of hand, then the dreamer is going to be the subject of scandal. An American almanac says that to see someone being hurt at a party is an omen of a long life; though a recent British source has suggested that a recurring dream of being at parties is a warning against overindulgence.

PATCHES
Dreams of patched clothing have been noted for almost five centuries, and the authorities are agreed that this is another dream of contrary — the more patches, the better the future looks. To dream of patching children's clothes was said to warn of sickness, while the young girl who dreamed of patches on her dress was keeping secrets from her lover. A lot of brightly coloured patches are an encouragement to speculate or have a gamble, according to a recent British source — which adds that to dream of someone wearing an eyepatch foretells an unusual sexual experience!

PAWNSHOP
The pawnshop has featured in dreams for several centuries, although they attracted most attention in Victorian studies where they were generally described as omens of contrary. To dream of going to a pawnshop was said to presage an improvement in finances; while to pawn an item would result in the end of a worrying problem. A married

169

woman who imagined going to a pawnship, however, was said by one early twentieth-century source to be guilty of an indiscretion; while any young girl who dreamed of being unable to reclaim a pawned item was being deceived by her lover.

PEARLS

The omens concerning pearls, seen in dreams, vary considerably. In Europe they are said to presage wealth and a rise in social position, though in America they are believed to represent tears and unhappiness. In many parts of the world it is regarded as bad luck to dream of losing or breaking a string of pearls — but in America it is a sign of making new friends! A woman who dreams of receiving a gift of pearls has a faithful lover and will make a good marriage.

PEAS

Most nations regard peas as symbolic of good health and prosperity. Rural almanacs claim that to plant peas is a sign the dreamer's plans are well grounded and will be realised. In Europe, since the Middle Ages, to dream of peas growing has been a sign of good fortune, and to dream of picking and shelling them indicates a recovery from illness. This is not quite true in America, however, for there the woman who has this dream will apparently find her partner less than satisfactory at lovemaking! A recent British survey has also suggested that to dream of opening a can of peas is symbolic of revealing a lot of little problems.

PENIS

Dreams of the male sex organ have been reported by both sexes, and are said by the authorities to be symbolic of the dreamer's attitudes. For a woman to have a recurring dream of the penis is an indication she is seeking a more fulfilling relationship. For a man to dream of his own sex organ is a sign of a good love-life, although if he imagines having any kind of problem with his penis, then this is a warning against overindulgence. A dream of exposing the sex organ is symbolic of sexual frustration.

PERFUME
Dreams of perfume were first reported in the Far East, where to imagine inhaling a delicate scent was a sign of happiness. The Romans believed to dream of having perfume on clothes was symbolic of power and admiration; and the French have for centuries maintained that to imagine smelling perfume indicates an exciting new love-affair. To drop or spill perfume presages the loss of something much cherished by the dreamer. Victorian almanacs sniffishly declared that the man who dreamed of perfume could expect misunderstanding in both business and personal affairs. A recent American almanac says the woman who dreams of preferring a special perfume is cheating in love-affairs; while the man who imagines putting perfume on a woman is about to commit adultery.

PETTICOATS
Dreams of petticoats have been reported since the sevententh century, and are considered to be symbolic of romantic affairs. European sources, in particular, said the young girl who dreamed of wearing a new petticoat would soon have a new lover, though to imagine a petticoat falling down at a social gathering, or while out walking, could lead to the loss of a lover. To be without a petticoat — or wearing a dirty and torn one — was believed to foretell seduction. Modern authorities think any dream of a petticoat is a warning against extravagance and vanity.

PHOTOGRAPHY
Although only invented in the early nineteenth century, a strong tradition of dreams about photography is now on record. One hundred years ago, a dream of a photograph was said to be 'a sign of approaching deception', while for

the dreamer to imagine having his or her picture taken 'foretells that you will unwarily cause yourself and others trouble'. A recent American source has suggested that to dream of looking at photographs forecasts the renewal of an old friendship; but to be taking them is a warning against speculation. A British source has added that if the dreamer cannot identify a face on a picture, then he or she is about to meet that person in real life!

PIANO
Another comparatively modern invention which also has a prominent place in dream lore and is said to symbolise happy occasions and general prosperity — when played joyfully. However, German almanacs state that a broken piano portends dissatisfaction, and an out of tune instrument means disappointment. If the music being played is either discordant or sad, then bad news is on the way. According to American sources, to see family or relatives playing a piano indicates arguments, and to dream of selling a piano points to a lonely old age. A British source also claims that to hear a piano being beautifully played is a promise of financial improvement.

PICTURES
Dreams in which pictures, such as watercolours or oils, have featured are generally considered good omens. Noted since the sixteenth century — primarily in Europe — the experiences foretell some welcome benefits, perhaps a financial windfall, or an improved love life. The Victorians, curiously, had reservations about dreams of paintings, feeling they indicated deception, and that to buy one foretold a worthless speculation. One book claimed that to have a dream of a group of old masters indicated 'insatiable longings' — though for what or whom it did not specify. An American authority states that pictures in general are symbolic of pleasure, though to dream of paintings in which nudes appear is a warning against scandalous behaviour.

PIGS

Pigs have been good omens in dreams since the Middle Ages, when they were first said to be symbols of prosperity. Rural almanacs claimed that fat and healthy pigs promised successful dealings; though if the animals appeared to be wallowing in mud then the dreamer should take notice of the advice of friends. A nineteenth-century European source said that any young girl who dreamed of pigs would end up with a jealous and greedy man, while most modern authorities are agreed that the pig symbolises making a good living.

PIGEONS

A flying pigeon has been seen as symbolic of receiving a long-distance message, according to documents on dreams that go back as far as the Roman Empire. White pigeons, in particular, are said to be omens of domestic happiness, and to see a group of these birds perching is a good sign for love-affairs. In Europe, to imagine shooting pigeons is a caution about business dealings, as the dreamer's ruthlessness could well be turned against him. British almanacs have claimed that pigeons seen on the ground are a warning about family squabbles, and to dream of feeding the birds points to an annoying financial problem which will take a little while to resolve.

PINE FORESTS

Scandinavian folklore has for centuries claimed that the pine tree is a symbol of long life and contentment, and research has also pointed to this being true in dreams. Authorities are agreed that to see a pine forest points to a family reunion, and that there is nothing ill-omened about cutting down pine trees for this signifies securing a congenial job. Throughout Europe, pine cones are believed to signify some unexpected good news — probably a birth. American sources say that any dream of pine furniture indicates a happy love-affair. Another recent report has also suggested the dream symbolises the benefits of a more healthy, open-air life.

PIRACY
Eighteenth-century almanacs are full of references to pirates, and though the dream is less noted today, the act of piracy in one form or another has been reported in various surveys. Two hundred years ago a dream of pirates was said to be a warning against the machinations of enemies, while the young girl who had this experience — especially being captured by pirates — was in danger of being lured into a life of sin. Modern authorities are divided on dreams about piracy: on the one hand it is considered a warning against being deceived in money matters; on the other it counsels caution in any new venture, and particularly to make sure of the financial viability of associates.

PLANETS
A number of the earliest science fiction books were based on dreams the authors had of journeys to planets like Mars and Venus; and, indeed, since the days of the ancient Greeks such experiences have been described as symbolic of a long and uncomfortable journey. Early European almanacs warned these dreamers not to be too superstitious, although by the Victorian era the definition had been revised to signify an unreachable objective. Modern authorities feel that any dream of the planets is another instance of inner conflict reflecting a need for change.

PLANTS
Plants in dreams are believed to be a fairly obvious guide to the future. If they are healthy and flourishing, then current plans will go well; if they are wilting and dying, then problems can be expected. Rural almanacs claim that plants in bloom signify a financial benefit, while to dream of watering a plant indicates a birth in the family. In the broadest terms, authorities agree that plants signify a happy homelife.

POISON
The ancients were fascinated by dreams of poisoning, and predictably saw them as ill-omened. The Romans, for example, believed that to dream of being poisoned was a warning that others were plotting against the sleeper; while to administer poison was a caution about acts that would alienate relatives and friends. In the Middle Ages, the lover who dreamed of poisoning a rival would soon be separated from his or her loved one because of jealousy, and to poison animals would result in family troubles. The Victorians feared that anyone who dreamed of poisoning could expect trouble from an unexpected source, though to imagine others poisoned indicated a release from worries. Modern authorities suggest the dream results from stressful tension, which may have been caused through false accusations or an unwillingness to compromise on a matter of principle.

POLICEMEN
Dreams in which policemen feature are not the omens of trouble that may be imagined. Indeed, modern authorities are agreed that the police symbolise security, and even to imagine being arrested is actually a dream of contrary: help from an unexpected source will soon enable the dreamer to solve a difficult problem. In Europe, books of dream lore are a little more sceptical, believing that to see policemen signifies some dramatic fluctuations in affairs; while in America, the same dream presages an embarrassment brought about by someone else's financial carelessness. A recent survey has also suggested that the dream may be a pointer to being trapped in a routine, from which it would be wise to try to escape.

POLITICS
A century ago a dream of a politician was said to presage 'displeasing companionships', while to engage in political arguments indicated misunderstandings and falling out

with friends! Today, to dream of politics is seen more as a pointer to resolving a current problem successfully — unless, say several authorities, the dream involved an argument with a member of the opposite sex. In this case, be warned against putting too much effort into a project, which will prove doomed to failure.

POTATO
As one of the staple foods of life, it is perhaps no surprise to learn that for centuries dreams about the potato have been seen as symbolic of stability in the home. In the Middle Ages, to dream of digging up potatoes indicated success based on hard work, though if any of them were rotten the future was bleak. By and large, eating potatoes cooked in any manner is viewed by modern writers as a sign of realising some plans; though the French believe that to peel potatoes indicates the arrival of an unwelcome guest. An amusing Australian almanac said recently that the man who dreamed of frying potatoes would soon fall for the charms of a buxom woman!

PREGNANCY
The omens for dreams of pregnancy have varied considerably over the years. For several centuries, the woman who dreamed of being with child was said to be receiving a premonition of the event; but 300 years ago, this view was revised to indicate that the dreamer was unhappy with her husband. A single girl who imagined being pregnant was in danger of seduction, and would remain unmarried for some time. The consensus of modern authorities is that any woman who dreams of being pregnant is about to enjoy a financial windfall. However, the man who sees himself getting a woman pregnant is being warned against promiscuity.

PRINCE
Since the Middle Ages, any dream of a prince or princess has been seen as a sign of a better lifestyle with improved

prospects. The early almanacs spoke of meeting a prince as indicating receiving a present; while to have an audience with a prince or princess would lead to success in business deals. Victorian books of dream lore considered it a very good omen to dream of talking to a prince, as this presaged a new circle of influential friends, while doing the same with a princess would lead to a very beneficial marriage. Modern surveys suggest dreams of this kind are an unconscious desire for self-esteem, which could actually be achieved by being more relaxed and sociable.

PROSTITUTE
Harlots featured in several of the earliest works on dream lore and were condemned then, as they were for many centuries afterwards, as a symbol of ruination. In the Middle Ages, dreams of these women were said to indicate sickness and poverty, and the Victorians informed any man who dreamed of going with a prostitute that he was risking the scorn of his family and friends for his indiscretions. Modern writers are agreed that the dream symbolises fears of sexual inadequacy, though the man who sees himself being solicited is receiving a warning about falling prey to the flattery of women. An amusing American survey has also reported recently that the man who dreams of a night with a very obliging prostitute can expect to be faced with a very bad business situation soon after!

PUBLIC HOUSE
Dreams of English public houses have been reported for several centuries, and although a few nineteenth-century writers claimed the experience was a warning against 'some questionable mode of advancement', others have believed it to be symbolic of a need for friendship. Several modern authorities believe that to dream of being in a bar with friends indicates the dreamer is more highly thought of than he or she may realise; while if the people are relatives, 'exciting times are ahead'. A British source has also

claimed that any dream featuring a public house is actually a suggestion to the dreamer to become more involved in community matters.

PUNISHMENT
To be punished or chastised in a dream is one of the classic contrary experiences. Indeed, accounts from the Middle Ages relate that dreamers who imagined themselves being flogged could actually look forward to an unexpected pleasure; and to see others being punished signified receiving news from someone who had been absent. Victorian sources were strangely quiet on this topic, although one did claim that any dream of punishment was a warning against unjustifiable jealousy. Today's consensus of opinion says that to dream of punishment indicates a forthcoming event of which the dreamer will be proud.

Q

QUACK DOCTOR
The quack doctor with his potions and lotions has had a place in dream lore since the seventeenth century, where he has been listed as a symbol of suspicion. One of the earliest references stated that to see a quack doctor presaged an illness that would be incorrectly diagnosed and treated. A nineteenth-century American source declared that to dream of a quack indicated a change of surroundings, although a contemporary European source thought it more likely that the sleeper was becoming morbid over some problems, and should work hard to overcome them. A recent report has suggested the implication is to be careful about accepting new friends at face value.

QUAGMIRE
To dream of falling into a quagmire terrified the sleeping hours of Europeans in the seventeenth and eighteenth centuries, and the fact it was symbolic of struggling to meet obligations was not much comfort when they awoke. British sources of the same period stated that to see another person struggling in a quagmire indicated that the dreamer's life was going to be affected by the failures of others. This oppressive dream has continued to be reported, and opinions now believe it to be a warning of impending ill-health.

179

QUARRELLING

A common feature in dreams since records were started, and now almost universally held to be a case of contrary. Although some Roman sources suggested that a dream of quarrelling with relatives or friends portended unhappiness, this definition was superseded by the conviction that it meant a happy home life and reunions with friends. For the last 300 years, to dream of starting a quarrel has indicated prosperity, especially in business; while to argue with a member of the family will result in the quick resolution of everyday problems. Only a quarrel with a complete stranger has a catch to it, according to modern sources, for this signifies a change of residence.

QUAY

Eighteenth-century English mariners believed a dream of standing alone on a quay was very ill-omened, for it signified grief and loss of life at sea. In later years, almanac writers claimed that any dream of a quay presaged a long journey; though if there were vessels alongside the dreamer could rest happy that his objectives would be achieved. A recent American book of dream lore says that a quay bustling with life is a good sign for business, but one that is idle or neglected is an omen of disappointment, probably for matters of the heart.

QUEEN

To see a queen in a dream is regarded as a lucky sign almost everywhere, especially if any kind of journey was undertaken during the experience. Since the early part of the nineteenth century, the dream also augured well for any ventures the dreamer might pursue. Some sources added that a monarch who looked old and haggard indicated unhappiness associated with forthcoming social activities. Curiously, in America the omens are reversed: dreaming of a queen is said to indicate deceit in love-affairs; while any kind of meeting with a monarch points to a 'rebellion in the home'.

QUESTIONS
To dream of answering questions is an omen of good luck — as long as the answers are correct. If they are persistently wrong, then this is symbolic of a failure to face up to the challenges of life. Victorian almanacs reported that to dream of questioning the merit of things indicated dissatisfaction with work or a feeling of being cheated in love by a member of the opposite sex. These same sources said that to imagine being persistently questioned in a dream was a warning about being treated in an underhand way by business associates. The happiest dream concerns children, for if they are asking questions then the dreamer is about to receive some good news.

QUEUE
Standing in a queue is hardly one of life's most enjoyable pastimes, unless the objective of the wait is worthwhile; and in dream lore this experience is symbolic of obtaining knowledge. In both Britain and America during the hard days of the 1920s and 1930s, a dream of queuing was said to result in being reunited with an old friend. In Europe, the girl who imagines being in a queue is in line for getting married; while in Australia the sleeper who sees a long queue of people is being warned that he or she is the subject of gossip-mongers.

QUICKSAND
The sensation of falling into a quicksand has been regarded since medieval times as symbolic of temptation. The dreamer who ends up in a quicksand is being warned about sinking into deceitful activities, particularly in relation to the opposite sex. Victorian sources believed the dream to indicate a slide into immorality; though young ladies were encouraged to higher things with the incentive that if they

dreamed of rescuing a lover from a quicksand, they would be rewarded with a worthy and faithful husband. Modern authorities believe the dream may well be a warning against prying into the affairs of other people.

QUILL
Despite the fact that using a quill pen was a laborious way of writing, the implement became symbolic of 'rushing trade' to quote a 350-year-old dream almanac which believed it represented prosperity and success. Victorian sources claimed that to dream of a quill denoted literary achievement to those who were so inclined; while a young woman who imagined wearing one on her hat would charm an array of admirers. Modern authorities prefer to believe that plucking or using a quill will produce good luck, as a result of receiving some important information.

QUOITS
This ancient game has been accorded many different omens over the years, and after a long association with bad luck it is now more closely linked with love and happiness. Two hundred years ago, to dream of playing the game was said to put a man in danger of losing his job, while a woman might well find herself homeless! In America, at the turn of the century, quoits were said to be symbolic of loneliness and trouble, presaging disagreeable work for women, and many arguments for men. A more recent study of the dream, however, has concluded that it more likely pertains to love-affairs, and that to 'ring' one of the targets will result in meeting an exciting new partner.

R

RABBIT

The rabbit is generally thought of in European dream lore as an omen of good luck; but recently in Australia, it has come to symbolise hard times for many rural areas of the continent, which are in danger of being overrun. Old British almanacs state that to dream of a number of rabbits indicates prosperity, while white rabbits denote faithfulness in love. A century ago, American sources believed the sight of rabbits running pointed to a change of occupation, though to eat one would lead to a quarrel with a friend. A recent Australian survey concluded that dreaming of shooting a rabbit was a sign of happiness, although an English book of dream lore says the sight of domestic rabbits signifies an increase in responsibilities.

RACING

The ancient Greeks, with their great passion for sport, first noted dreams of racing, although they only partially associated them with athletics. According to documents, to dream of being in a race was believed to be symbolic of other people aspiring to what the dreamer was working to possess; although as long as he imagined winning he could be sure of ultimate success. With the passage of time, this experience has been classified as an obstacle dream regardless of whether the sleeper is taking part or watching, the

183

result being crucial to the omens. European sources believe the dream can also symbolise an exciting new venture; while a recent American authority concluded it was an incentive to persevere in order to achieve recognition.

RAGGED

The nobility in Roman times were said to be particularly concerned about dreams in which they or other people they knew appeared in ragged garments, as these were said to be symbolic of social disgrace and unhappiness. The people of the Middle Ages equally believed that to see people washing rags or children dressed in dirty and torn clothes were omens of strife. The Victorian preoccupation with dress is well recorded, and one almanac of the time stated that the young girl who dreamed of wearing rags would fall into the clutches of an arrogant man; while a contemporary French source declared that a dream of a rag-picker would lead to a rise in status. Modern authorities believe this dream is a warning about moral behaviour, or alternatively a need to work harder in order to avoid poverty.

RAILWAYS

Since the late nineteenth century, the railway has been seen as symbolic of travel, with some good fortune thrown in. Victorian almanacs said that to dream of riding on a railway signified some exciting social events ahead; though to imagine walking along the track was a pointed suggestion not to ignore the demands of business. In the early 1900s an American source believed that any train journey, especially one with children, presaged a period of domestic bliss.

RAIN

Although it may not be much fun to be caught in a downpour of rain, to dream of it falling is a good omen. Some of the earliest dream records speak of rain as symbolic of 'blessings descending', and for at least 400 years to imagine being in a storm presaged an unexpected financial windfall.

Victorian sources declared that to see rain through a window indicated marital joy, though any which leaked through into a building was a sign that 'illicit pleasure will come to you rather unexpectedly'! Some modern sources feel that a heavy downpour is also symbolic of the need to face up to a crisis. However they agree with the age-old tradition that a dream of a rainbow is a pointer to the end of a troubled period and a sign of happiness for lovers.

RANSOM
To dream of being held to ransom is another of the classic dreams of contrary: it indicates coming into some money. The Victorians, however, had certain reservations about this definition, and believed the dreamer was actually in danger of being deceived by people who were after his money. A modern American authority has claimed that the woman who imagines being held for ransom is looking for a more exciting sex life.

RAPE
Although records of dreams of rape are scant until the nineteenth century, there seems little doubt that for a woman to imagine being sexually assaulted was seen as a warning against behaviour which could be misinterpreted as an invitation to intimacy. Victorian almanacs were stern in their admonitions that any female who dreamed of rape would lose her lover and her reputation. A European authority feels any dream in which rape occurs is a warning that the dreamer is going to be shocked by the activities of a friend, while a recent British survey reported it to be a much more general caution against giving false impressions to other people. A German book on dream lore has added that the man who dreamed of being raped by a woman was going to come into an unexpected inheritance!

RATS
In China and ancient Egypt the rat was regarded as the god

of plague (despite the fact that it is a flea carried by the rat which actually transmits the destructive epidemic), and dreams of the rodent were therefore believed to symbolise that the dreamer was in danger of sickness. In the Middle Ages, dreams of rats were said to presage being deceived and injured by neighbours, although to kill a rat would mean a small triumph over enemies. Victorian almanacs declared that plagues of rats foretold serious domestic problems, while a recent American source suggested that to dream of catching a rat foretold being caught by an energetic lover! In fact, because of the shape of the rat's muzzle, some dream researchers have ascribed a phallic significance to it; although the abhorrence in which the rodent is held by mankind has led to it being seen as symbolising unwelcome sex, probably rape.

READING
To dream of reading has been increasingly reported this century, and is said to be symbolic of progress and excelling at work. Victorian almanacs believed such a dream would 'cultivate literary abilities', although a European authority writing at the time of World War I maintained that seeing others reading was a sign of having good friends. A recent American book of dream lore claims that dreaming of reading aloud is a sign of future changes; while to dream of reading but not understanding something is a warning about losing some money through a hasty decision.

RECEPTION
Attending a reception can be an unnerving experience and the omens of dreaming about one are also mixed. The earliest records of this dream (from France), declared that it simply foretold a 'pleasant engagement', but eighteenth-century European sources tempered this by stating that anything untoward which happened at the reception meant some social problems were looming. An American authority has written that to dream of giving a reception

186

points to a rise in social status, although to be the centre of attention at one is a warning about being vain.

RECORDS
It is an everyday occurrence for some to dream of being a recording star, although to have the same experience while asleep is symbolic of increased social activity. European authorities believe that to dream of listening to records is a warning against being taken in by flattering words; while to imagine buying them is also a caution against extravagance. A British source suggested recently that to dream of a record player or tape recorder is the first sign that a love-affair is failing.

REFEREE
To dream of a referee in any sport has a quite different omen depending on which side of the Atlantic the reader lives. In Europe, the experience is a warning that the subject is taking sport too seriously, and should enjoy it more. In America it presages being treated unfairly on a matter of principle. A suggestion by an Australian book of dream lore, that to imagine being an actual referee is symbolic of enjoying a quiet and pleasant life, may not be intended to be taken all that seriously!

REPTILES
Attacks by reptiles have featured in dreams since Roman times, and although they presage danger this can be prevented if the creature is killed. The earliest records state that to dream of a reptile, such as a snake, indicated having hidden enemies. Even if the dreamer caught the creature alive, he or she would still be the subject of slanderous remarks. European sources are no fonder of reptiles: in France a dead one is suggestive of disputes; while in Spain to see one in captivity is a warning to be careful in business deals. A recent British source has claimed a sexual connotation for reptiles: a girl who dreams of a number of them

has rivals for the affection of her lover — and if she is bitten, she will lose her man.

RESCUE
Another of the famous dreams of contrary: being rescued by someone means misfortune is looming; while to rescue another person indicates business losses. In the eighteenth century a dream of rescuing someone from drowning was read as a personal message not to go to sea, and Victorian almanacs informed readers that saving a relative would lead to big family arguments. Modern authorities feel this dream is a warning that the dreamer is about to experience an accident-prone period in life, and should take great care.

REVENGE
People at all stages of history have dreamed of revenge, both figuratively and literally, and the earliest records indicate that the omens were symbolic of humiliation. In the Middle Ages any dream of taking revenge was believed to presage anxious times ahead, and to imagine oneself personally exacting revenge was a sign to be very careful of enemies. Victorian almanacs believed the dream to be symbolic of a 'weak and uncharitable nature' which should be controlled, and the man who dreamed of taking revenge on a rival suitor would find it difficult to attract another lover. Today's authorities believe the dream to signify a narrow-minded approach to problems.

RICE
The Chinese have always thought that dreams of rice symbolised prosperity and happiness, although in the West, firm friendships have been substituted for the latter, with just a note of caution to take care in making plans. Far Eastern sources indicate that farmers who dreamed of large rice crops would have no domestic problems, but dirty or impure rice grains signified illness. To eat rice with others is regarded as a good omen world-wide, and the young girl

who dreams of making a rice dish will soon be serving a family of her own. Some modern authorities believe a dream of rice fields signifies the moment is right to fulfil a long-standing obligation.

RING
The ring has been a dream symbol for centuries and is most widely accepted as a sign of love. The Romans believed that to dream of being given a ring or finding one indicated a new lover; and in the Middle Ages there are the first records of a broken ring signifying unhappiness and separation. In nineteenth-century Europe to dream of rings studded with precious stones pointed to wealth — or perhaps the birth of a child — and to notice rings on other people foretold new friendships. Some modern writers have claimed that losing a ring in a dream will lead to success in business dealings.

RIVER
Rivers in dreams are like life, following their own course, and the many different images of them seen in sleep are said to be like the vicissitudes of destiny. In the ancient Egyptian and Arabic dream books, for instance, the size of the river was believed to represent the greater or lesser importance of the dreamer's destiny, while the Romans added that a clear, smoothly flowing river symbolised prosperity and happiness in family matters; and a muddy, turbulent stretch pointed to disagreements and petty jealousies. European authorities believe that to dream of falling in a river is a warning against hasty actions, while to walk along the bank signifies the future is looking good. In America, a flooding river is said to indicate lawsuits; a small river is symbolic of wasting money; and to dream of fishing in a river foretells a change of environment. A recent British source has also claimed this dream is symbolic of drifting along in life, when a real effort would achieve worthwhile and lasting success.

189

ROADS

It is not surprising to find the first dreams about roads recorded by those fine highway builders, the Romans, who believed they symbolised destiny. They agreed that a smooth, straight road was the path to happiness and prosperity; that a rough and twisting road presaged trials and tribulation; and the farther the road stretched ahead in the dream, the longer the sleeper would live. Medieval writers were concerned that a winding road across hostile terrain indicated numerous obstacles in life; though if this became straight and wide at any point, then a financial gain could be expected. Seventeenth-century European sources agreed that to lose sight of the road boded ill for trade, and that to be in the company of strangers was a warning against robbery. Twentieth-century almanacs have suggested that any signs seen alongside a dream road indicate some small but pleasant changes in the subject's social life.

ROBBERY

Some time during the Middle Ages, dreams of being robbed were defined as cases of contrary, so that the dreamer who imagined losing his valuables in a robbery could actually look forward to an increase in wealth. Some sources even suggested that to be attacked by robbers signified success in trade. But, if a robber was seen running away (said a French authority) then the dreamer was about to suffer a disappointment in love! Modern research has suggested that a dream of being robbed of money is a warning to be more careful in financial matters.

ROBIN

That most delightful of little songbirds with its distinctive red breast, which is found in Europe, parts of Asia and Africa, has been considered an omen of good fortune for centuries. In the sixteenth century, European sources were first to credit it with symbolising happiness in family life, and in Asia dreams of the bird are believed to presage the arrival of good news from afar. African folklore adds that dreams of the bird foretell the birth of sons who will become the leaders of men; while in Britain to see the robin on the wing points to making a new friend.

ROCKS

A classic obstacle dream noted throughout Europe, and which symbolises difficulties and hard work. In earlier times rocks were said to indicate enemies, and unless the obstructions were climbed over or removed, then the dreamer's life was in danger. From the eighteenth-century, to climb up a steep rock foretold disappointments in domestic affairs; while difficulty in getting down would mean the death of a friend. Modern sources are agreed that to dream of falling rocks is a sign of changes in life, and the general symbolism of the dream is an appeal to the dreamer not to allow himself to be defeated by obstacles.

ROOF

Dreams about roofs have actually changed very little over the centuries, despite buildings becoming taller as well as better constructed. Early almanacs indicated that to dream of standing on a roof symbolised reaching the heights of success, though to have the sensation of falling off indicated the achievement would be short-lived. A roof caving in was a warning against a sudden calamity; while a dream of a leaking roof foretold a loss of money or possibly of sexual powers. Seventeenth-century sources claimed that to imagine installing a new roof was a pointer to good times ahead. Interestingly, several recent almanacs have claimed a roof on fire is actually an encouragement to the dreamer that his worst fears will not be realised!

ROOM

Only dreams of strange rooms have any significance, for in familiar surroundings it will be another of the elements

observed by the dreamer that will prove crucial in determining the omens. From the Middle Ages, a richly furnished room was said to foretell 'a sudden fortune' for a
man; and for a girl, a meeting with a wealthy stranger who
would offer her marriage. Small and poorly furnished
rooms were defined in the seventeenth century as symbols
of sickness and poverty, although sometimes they might
lead to the discovery of a family secret. Some modern
authorities have suggested the dream has sexual connotations: a strange room alluding to the secrecy of an extra-
marital affair; and a small one presaging the claustrophobia
engendered by the deceit necessary for such an affair.

ROPES

The rope has been another symbol recorded since biblical
times, and believed to indicate complications in human
affairs. Early sources said a dream of making a rope would
lead to the solution of a difficult problem; while to climb up
one would enable the dreamer to outwit enemies. In the
Middle Ages, to be tied up with a rope foretold a difficult
entanglement with a member of the opposite sex, and to
walk along a rope warned against a hazardous speculation.
The Victorian almanacs declared that a number of ropes
tangled together signified the dreamer was being deceived,
but to untangle them pointed to a new start in life. Modern
sources agree that the rope is a symbolic invitation to 'climb
up in life'.

ROSES

Beautiful roses have always been seen as signs of happiness, especially in matters of love. The earliest records note
that a young girl who dreamed of picking roses would soon
have an offer of marriage, though roses that were withering
were a sign of deceit by a lover. The Victorians prized red
roses as symbols of honour and vitality, though to dream of
white roses was an omen of illness. Modern sources agree

that to dream of receiving a gift of roses is symbolic of being loved both physically and spiritually.

RUNNING

The dream of running is one of the most famous on record, and although authorities over the centuries have applied many omens to it, the experience is now universally accepted to symbolise a need to escape from a difficult or embarrassing situation. Coupled with this is a feeling of being unable to run — or else not fast enough to reach the required destination in time — which researchers believe indicates a lack of self-confidence in tackling the problem. In much earlier times, it was suggested that a dream of running away from danger signified a fear of losing trade or wealth — which became certain if the dreamer stumbled or fell. In the seventeenth century, a young girl who dreamed of running was said to be afraid of losing her virginity; while several European almanacs believed that for a man, it meant he was afraid of banishment or exile from his native land. An eighteenth-century dream book declared that to imagine running in circles was symptomatic of the sleeper believing friends despised him; and to run naked indicated a fear of being robbed by relatives! The Victorians claimed that a dream about a lot of people running around, in wild confusion, heralded bad news; and that the dreamer who felt rooted to the spot was about to become ill — a diagnosis still accepted today.

S

SADNESS
Ancient documents indicate that the Arabs and Chinese were deeply influenced by dreams in which strong feelings of sadness manifested themselves, and it was they who first believed the omens pointed to good fortune. Some authorities have claimed this was one of the very first dreams to be labelled a case of contrary: clear sign that the dreamer's troubles would soon be over. The Greeks believed it signified 'lasting joy' and if more than one member of a family was involved then good times were prophesied. Only one exception to this rule is on record — in America — where a number of sources have stated that to dream of relatives being sad presages a family quarrel.

SAFE
A safe is regarded as a symbol of security, and several Victorian almanacs claimed the dream augured well for businessmen who were worried about set-backs in their professions. To dream of struggling to open a safe, however, signifies that certain plans may not come to fruition; while an empty safe confirms that problems lie ahead. Recently, some British and American researchers have suggested this could be another dream of contrary, and that to unlock a safe full of valuables foretells a bundle of troubles.

SAILING
Just as sailing can be a great pleasure in fine weather on calm waters, so to dream of this activity symbolises pleasure and happiness. The Greeks established the original idea that the weather was crucial to the omens, and the dreamer could be either on board the boat or merely observing sails from a distance. Bad weather and turbulent seas predict disappointment. Books of dream lore also agree that to be a sailor indicates a sense of restlessness, and a long journey or important news from overseas is imminent. American sources have added that to dream of raising a sail is a good luck sign, though if other people are doing this, then a love-affair is in jeopardy.

SALT
The Romans placed a high value on salt, and believed that to dream about it was a good sign which symbolised abundant wealth. In the Middle Ages, documents indicate that a dream of being a salt merchant signified prosperity, although to be careless in its use would lead to family quarrels. Spilling salt was also said to indicate difficulties, though they would be short-lived. Modern authorities have suggested that dreaming of salt symbolises money which should be invested with care to ensure a secure future.

SAND
The earliest records of sand in dreams indicate it was felt to be symbolic of famine and losses. The Arabs, however, believed a sandstorm was an omen of contrary — bringing them long life — while to surmount an enormous sand dune indicated having many relatives and friends to rely upon. African folklore curiously maintains that to see a home being damaged by a sandstorm suggests the dreamer should build a new dwelling. Modern American almanacs believe that sand is symbolic of 'small vexations' which have resulted from indecision, although British sources

195

prefer the explanation that it is a warning against being exploited by new acquaintances.

SAPPHIRES
These beautiful blue gemstones have been seen as symbols of spiritual blessing since biblical times. According to the earliest dream records, they signify 'fortunate gain' for men, and a suitable lover for women. For at least 500 years, sapphires worn by others have been pointers to a rise in social status according to European sources, although in Asia they indicate disputes between friends. A British authority has written recently that to dream of wearing sapphires is also a warning against impulsive behaviour.

SCAFFOLD
According to medieval records, people drew comfort from dreams of someone being executed on the scaffold as they were said to foretell a long life! Curiously, however, it was thought that to dream of falling from a scaffold would lead to being exposed for plotting ill against others. As the hangman's scaffold disappeared from use, it became symbolic in dreams of losing the affection of a loved one; while in modern times it is said to indicate a serious blow to future prospects as a result of an indiscretion.

SCANDAL
Eighteenth century French romantic almanacs informed their readers that a dream of a scandal was a warning to young men to choose their companions more carefully, and to young women to beware the blandishments of *older* men. In Victorian England, the female who dreamed of discussing a scandal was laying herself open to seduction and was unlikely to enjoy the state of matrimony. Some American sources believe that there are contrary elements in this dream: for women it will actually be followed by a marriage proposal, while a man can expect financial gains. A recent British survey suggests that to dream of being involved in a

scandal means that the dreamer is nursing a secret regret, but if the scandal concerns others, then the dreamer's integrity is about to be challenged by a member of the opposite sex.

SCHOOL
For the past 300 years schools have been viewed as symbols of the simple pleasures and trusts of childhood, and any dream about a school is a subconscious desire to escape feelings of discontent about the present; especially if the dreamer imagined being back as a child in class. Nineteenth-century almanacs claimed that to dream of being in school signified a thirst for knowledge, and the feeling of being a teacher augured well for business prospects. Modern research thinks the dream is also symbolic of a reluctance to break with old associations which are, in fact, actually holding the dreamer back.

SCULPTOR
The Greeks believed a sculptor symbolised change, and to dream of one was an omen that the time was right to take up a fresh challenge. In the Middle Ages, the dream was regarded more cautiously as the change in life could prove more arduous and less rewarding. Of late, authorities have concentrated on the sculptor and his model: European sources suggesting that the woman who dreams of posing naked will realise her ambitions. An American book of dream lore claims that the virgin who poses for a sculptor will marry a rich man.

SEARCHING
The feeling of searching for something has been widely recorded in dream lore, and in most cases should be related to the article being sought. An eighteenth-century authority, however, believed this dream to be symbolic of infidelity, and to see a group of people searching meant the dreamer was the subject of gossip. Victorian almanacs

claimed searching was a caution against committing any act that might bring about family dishonour, though in Europe it was seen as a warning to watch out for thieves. A recent British researcher has concluded that the dreamer is being advised against wasting time on a meaningless pursuit or a doomed relationship.

SECRET

An amusing dream-survey published in Germany in 1980 claimed that in virtually every case where people had dreamt of being told a secret, they could not remember what it was on waking! Earlier writers believed that betraying a secret would result in divine punishment, although one Indian source suggested it would eventually lead to a substantial inheritance! Victorian almanacs informed dreamers that if they were told a secret they should learn to control their passions, but if they told someone else a secret it would lead to the end of a love-affair. Modern sources believe the dream to be an omen of gossip and intrigue.

SEEDS

Mankind has always been dependent on seeds, and dream lore believes them to be omens of growth and prosperity. The earliest writers insisted this dream was significant, no matter how unfavourable the conditions might be, and in families where the planting of seeds was the responsibility of others, the dream was said to be symbolic of a forthcoming wedding. Today, any dream in which seeds feature represents new opportunities which should be seized for a better and more fulfilling life.

SEWING

Since the Middle Ages, sewing has been viewed as symbolic of hard work, though to complete any piece of sewing in a dream foretells success in current undertakings. In the nineteenth century, to dream of sewing clothing indicated a period of domestic harmony, though it was a bad omen to dream of a seamstress, for she prophesied a death in the family. From the early 1900s, to dream of a sewing machine was said by European sources to be a caution about business affairs. Recent surveys have indicated that the very act of sewing is a warning to the dreamer to make sure he or she has adequately prepared for the future in the eventuality of hard times.

SEX

Sexual indulgence in dreams has been written about at great length in various studies, including the classic work by Sigmund Freud, the consensus of opinion pointing to them as symbolic of repression and/or frustration. The sex organs themselves have also been the subject of study: for men, diseased or deformed genitals are said to warn against overindulgence; while for either men or women to dream of having no sex organs is a pointer to seeking guidance about their sex life. Both men and woman have reported dreams of exposing their sexual organs, and these have been defined as a caution against committing indiscretions. Among the objects which are cited as common phallic symbols in dreams are guns, sticks, keys and tools. Female sexuality, on the other hand, is symbolised by boxes, rooms and pockets.

SHAMPOO

The act of shampooing the hair has an association with love and sex that goes back for several centuries. A nineteenth-century source, for example, claims euphemistically that those who dream of washing their own hair will soon have an exciting trip that they will enjoy, as long as they 'keep the real purpose from family or friends'! A curious 1919 almanac reports that to see another person being shampooed will make the dreamer indulge in 'undignified affairs to please others'. Modern authorities believe that to dream of shampooing another person's hair is symbolic of a vigorous and satisfactory sex life.

SHAVING

In general terms, dreams of shaving relate to business and finance for men, and matters of the heart for women. The earliest records indicate that a man who dreamed of being shaved would lose money through untrustworthy friends; while the woman who saw a man having his beard trimmed was contemplating infidelity. In the nineteenth century, to have a rough shave pointed to business failures; and the woman who dreamed of shaving her face would be rejected by men. A recent American source suggests that any man who dreams of shaving should not gamble; while the woman who shaves under her arms will be popular with the opposite sex because of her passionate nature!

SHOES

As far back as the days of the Romans, shoes in dreams were said to be pointers to what the future held. Tight sandals, for instance, indicated money problems, while comfortable ones presaged happiness in love. In Europe, dreaming of wooden shoes promised good trading, while leather boots indicated a good marriage. British authorities, however, claimed that if buckles or shoelaces came undone in a dream, then there would be family quarrels, and to dream of children's shoes indicated a change of home. Modern dream research says that smart and comfortable shoes are symbolic of financial security; shabby and down-at-heel shoes will lead to unhappiness in personal life; and to lose a pair of shoes indicates the dreamer is wasting time on unproductive matters.

SIGNATURE

Ever since medieval times, dreams in which signatures have featured have been described as symbolising the loyalty of friends. To witness the signing of a document signified financial gain, though if the person writing his name was a judge, or any member of the legal fraternity, then this was a warning to beware of the machinations of enemies. European authorities believe that a dreamer who signs his own name will have good health, while an American almanac stated that signing any official document was a caution to take care of the eyesight! A recent survey has added that the dream may simply be a warning to read an important agreement very carefully when it arrives.

SILK

Centuries ago the Chinese described silk as a fortunate omen indicating pride and luxury. European authorities followed this lead by declaring that dreams of the material signified profit and honour; and that people who dreamed of wearing silken garments had the highest aspirations. In the nineteenth century, women who dreamed of buying silken dresses were said to be in love, though to tear the dress or get it dirty would mean they were being deceived. Only black silk has ever been described as ill-omened, though it remains very popular. An unusual Victorian almanac claimed that the girl who dreamed of old silk would be 'wooed by a wealthy but elderly man'. Today, the girl who dreams of wearing silken underwear or a negligée will soon meet a passionate lover.

SINGING

Curiously, documents relating to the minstrels of the Middle Ages provided the first clues to the omens contained in dreams of singing. Then, such night visions were believed to symbolise happiness and good company, unless the singing was mournful or out of tune, in which case bad news of an absent relative or friend was foretold. Hearing love-songs was a partial instance of contrary, for the sleeper could expect a quarrel after such a dream, though it would not bring about the end of the affair. Ribald songs — claimed several early twentieth-century almanacs

— pointed to an illness; while hymns would enhance the dreamer's status among friends and associates.

SISTER
The omens concerning a dream about a sister have changed very little over the years. Authorities are agreed that a woman who dreams of her sister will shortly be involved in a domestic argument, though to a man his sister symbolises good fortune and emotional security. If there is more than one sister in a family, the omens of the dream can vary according to the circumstances, though most bear on the closeness of the relationships and the need for honesty in all situations.

SKIES
Any sky seen in a dream offers straightforward omens about the dreamer's future, for the old adage about 'storm clouds gathering' does indeed foretell a period of hardship and stress. The clearer the sky the better the prospects for happiness; although authorities are agreed that a totally grey sky signifies trustworthy friends. For several centuries, European sources maintained that a dream of a red sky predicted public disorder and rioting, and to imagine mysterious objects falling from the sky was a prophecy of war. Victorian almanacs claimed that dreamers who believed themselves to be floating in the sky, unsure whether they were awake or not, were in for a very painful illness. Modern authorities put it down simply to a desire for escape, and the fascination with the blue vastness symbolising a need to understand the mysteries of life.

SKIN
The terrible plagues which have struck mankind were undoubtedly influential on the omens which have become associated with dreams about the skin. Original sources state that dreams of pale or diseased skin indicate sickness is looming; while smooth and attractive skin points to good

health, particularly on a woman. In the Middle Ages, dreams of washing the skin were said to presage a death, and peeling skin signified problems in trade. These omens remained largely unchanged until a century ago, when research declared a pale skin meant emotional problems; fair skin indicated sexual enjoyment; and peeling skin suggested domestic unhappiness. An American survey has added that sunburned skin is a warning about being cheated by friends.

SLIMMING

Concern with shape and weight has been a preoccupation with men and women for centuries, and dreams of the figure and obesity can be found on record right back to Roman times and beyond. The earliest documents indicate that to dream of a shapely figure presaged pleasant social engagements for a man; while for the women of the time it was a case of contrary because dreaming of growing fat actually signified happiness in love and making a good marriage! In the Middle Ages, too, fatness was equated with wealth. Modern research has revised these ideas, and now a dream of successfully slimming is said to point to exciting developments in the dreamer's love-life.

SNAKE

The snake in dreams is now accepted as a phallic symbol, though the earliest authorities declared it to be an omen of evil, prophesying illness and treachery. To see a number of snakes writhing about presaged unease and sickness, while if they coiled around the dreamer or actually struck, then this was a warning about the machinations of enemies. Later European authorities claimed that snakes signified accidents, and only by killing them could the bad luck be avoided. In the early years of the nineteenth century it was first suggested that to handle a snake was a warning of being led astray sexually, and further study has confirmed the definition that a snake anywhere on the body is symbolic of sexual passions or repressions.

SNOW

Despite the problems that heavy snow can cause, in dreams it is a good omen — symbolising protection and preservation (of the earth) — especially if the dream occurs in one of the other seasons. In Scandinavia, for example, to dream of snow in the summer will produce a good harvest in the autumn for the farmer, excellent opportunities for the businessman in the winter, and a spring love-affair for a woman. European authorities believe that to dream of deep snow hints at good news, probably financial; while to imagine ski-ing with a stranger will result in a new love-affair. Dirty snow can be an omen of illness, according to British almanacs, and to dream of snowflakes falling will cause a lover's tiff. Melting snow is widely believed to foretell a period of introversion, soon turning into happiness.

SON

Parents have always dreamed of sons, and the authorities are agreed that while dreams of any form of achievement by the boy point towards a success in the future, any suggestions of trouble, problems, or danger will actually befall the dreamer. A nineteenth-century almanac puts it quite clearly, 'If your son is sick then it is on you that the illness will fall.' Similar encouragement is also to be found in European sources, where any parent who rescues a son from danger can expect to see him rise to a position of eminence. Only in America is a dream conversation with a son said to result in business losses!

SPIDER

Though spiders terrify many people, they are actually a good omen in dreams and symbolic of tenacity and patience. The spider's web has been associated with domestic happiness since medieval times, and to dream of the creature climbing points to achievements in trading; while if it is working busily on its web there will be a steady amassing of wealth. Perhaps surprisingly, to kill a spider in a dream will bring good news (for according to superstition this brings bad luck), though even more amazingly an American authority has described anyone who dreams of *eating* a spider as 'a very voluptuous person'! Modern research suggests that at its most fundamental the dream is an appeal to show patience in any current problems. Freudians, however, maintain the spider symbolises a terrifying mother seeking to keep her son from another, younger woman.

SPORT
Dreams of sporting activities do not necessarily refer to athletic prowess, according to recent dream research, but can equally relate to domestic and social accomplishments. The sensation of winning at any sport bodes well for relationships with other people, and even to suffer an injury will bring important news rather than pain. Of specific sports, football is good for business ventures, cricket for social engagements, athletics symbolises travel, and tennis meetings with the opposite sex. American sources have added that basketball signifies a varied and fulfilling sex life, while to take part in a boxing match will bring about the loss of a friend.

SPY
The sensation of spying on others, or being spied upon, has a long tradition in dream lore, and has been universally defined as a warning against impulsive or ill-advised behaviour. An interesting eighteenth-century French almanac claimed that to dream of being harassed by spies pointed to a feeling of unease which could lead to potentially dangerous quarrels. A Victorian book of dream lore says that a vision of being a spy 'denotes that you will make unfortunate ventures'. Modern research suggests

the dream is symbolic of a need for more adventure, but cautions about the risk of it being sought too dangerously.

STAIRS
Dreams of stairs are another very common feature in dream lore, the omens of which have varied over the centuries. Greek and Roman sources agreed that climbing up a stair or ladder symbolised a rise in rank or authority, though to descend would bring misfortune in domestic and/or business life. Later European authorities thought a broad staircase signified wealth; while falling down one indicated problems brought about by malice and envy. The idea that cimbing up a staircase augured well for love-affairs was first suggested in the eighteenth century. Freud later claimed the entire dream was one of sexual symbolism: the act of climbing symbolising erection, and the descent representing the diminution of the penis after orgasm — with the reverse being true for women.

STEALING
The Egyptians believed dreams of stealing to be particularly ill-omened, and for anyone of noble birth to steal something was a death sign. Later authorities followed this lead, though suggesting the outcome would be bad luck and loss of reputation. By the Middle Ages to dream of stealing clothes was said to affect business dealings. Victorian almanacs claimed that a dreamer who imagined being accused of stealing was getting a warning about being misunderstood in some forthcoming activity, while to accuse another person of stealing was a caution against hasty actions. The consensus of modern opinion is that the dream is advising care with money — although to be caught stealing has been said by a number of these authorities to be another case of contrary in which the omen indicates good luck.

STOCK MARKET

Recent surveys have reported a vastly increased number of dreams about the world's stock markets, and all have concluded that it is an ill-omened experience. In fact, to imagine gaining on the market signifies losses; and only if the dreamer's speculations come to nothing can he or she hope to benefit. An American almanac has suggested that to dream of being a member of the Stock Exchange is a pointer to the illness of a friend.

STORMS

Storms and gales are as ill-omened in dreams as they are in life, foretelling problems which can only be overcome by determination and strength of character. The earliest sources declared that a man who witnessed an approaching storm in his dream would have business worries, while a woman could expect to be separated from her husband or lover. Seventeenth-century authorities claimed that any storm over a building was a warning against the activities of enemies; while in Europe a gale was believed to signify an attack on the morals and fidelity of the dreamer. To see the passing of a storm before waking indicates that the problems will be transitory.

STRAW

Rural almanacs have for generations laid emphasis on the good omens associated with straw, for it is said to symbolise security and prosperity. The oldest sources claimed that a dream of bundling straw was a sign of good business deals, while a full barn pointed to a happy domestic life. To lie on straw foretold a birth, though to see straw burning was a warning against carelessness with money. And those delicious fruits, strawberries, are equal signs of good fortune in dreams, for they symbolise abundance and happiness and, if eaten, the possibility of a new love-affair.

STREAM

Another very commonplace dream which the Romans declared to be symbolic of the flow of life. The stream that flows clear and tranquil through pleasant countryside points to a long and happy life for the dreamer. A winding and obstructed stream foretells a life of hard work, and one not without its problems. Seventeenth-century almanacs warned dreamers who imagined walking in a stream to beware of enemies, and that to fall in the water was a caution against actions which could bring about public disgrace.

STREETS

The streets of ancient Rome probably inspired the first dreams of this kind, and the fact they were wide and open has made such public highways symbolic of prosperity. The muddy and crowded streets of the towns and cities of the Middle Ages may just as easily have given rise to the idea of bad luck and worry being associated with thoroughfares of that kind. More recently it has been argued that winding streets prophesy travel, long streets a need for patience, and strange streets indicate new ventures. To be in any street and feel afraid, say modern authorities, is a suggestion the dreamer is contemplating an activity that may well prove dangerous.

SUN

Although the sun was symbolically described in earliest traditions as depicting either masculinity or femininity, the Arabic dream books believed it represented *both* the father and the mother; and was therefore a very good omen indeed. Roman sources thought the sun shining from a clear sky foretold family peace and harmony, though nothing but trouble would result from seeing a sun that was dark or stained by blood. By the Middle Ages, the sun was regarded as a symbol of progress and growth; and shortly afterwards as symbolising the development of consciousness and intelligence. In other words — the opening of doors to new opportunities and challenges in life. Modern study believes a dream of the sun promises exciting changes for the better.

SWANS
In Europe, swans have been regarded as omens of happiness for many centuries, though in Australia to dream of a black swan is believed to be a sign of bad luck, particularly in business matters. From the sixteenth century, dreams in which these majestic birds were seen flying were said to indicate prosperity. To see one of them injured was a warning to the sleeper against becoming self-satisfied and complacent. American sources have stated that swans seen on a pond can lead to the solving of a mystery. All the major authorities agree that to dream of killing a swan points to the break-up of a home and family.

SWIMMING
It is difficult to trace the first recorded instances of dreams about swimming, but certainly in France in the seventeenth century they were being described as symbolic of success in life — as long as the dreamer experienced no sensations of discomfort while in the water. European sources believed that swimming towards a shore pointed to overcoming problems, but moving away from it was a clear sign of having lost the sense of direction in life. British books of dream lore state that the location of the swim can be important in divining the omens — such as whether it is in the sea, in a river or in a swimming pool — and agree that the dream is also an incentive to pursue objectives with single-minded dedication.

T

TABLE

The table is a common dream symbol, though it is what appears on it that is crucial to the omens. The Romans decided that a table set with food and wine was a sign of prosperity, while one that was empty or broken signified hardship and disagreements. In the Middle Ages, a banqueting table indicated enjoyment; though to see any table being cleared was a warning that good times were about to be followed by bad. Nineteenth-century sources claimed that a kitchen table symbolised hard work; a dining table more social engagements; while a card table was a hint to take a gamble. A dirty tablecloth is also said to be a pointer to a family argument.

TAILOR

Medieval sources were the first to suggest that a dream about a tailor indicated an unexpected journey, probably brought about by a family problem. A seventeenth-century almanac claimed that the girl who dreamed of a tailor would marry beneath herself; though the man who had this dream should take especial care in business deals. In Europe, to be measured by a tailor presages a quarrel. Modern authorities have suggested that this dream is a warning about confiding too freely in people outside the family circle.

TALISMAN

The ancient Egyptians were intrigued by dreams in which talismans appeared, and believed they were symbolic of receiving gifts or favours. Old documents from Europe, however, claim they are omens of deception: a woman who dreams of a talisman should beware of a smooth-tongued seducer, while a man is in danger of being cheated by a friend. In Asia, to dream of a talisman points to solving a mystery; and in America the girl who dreams of wearing a talisman will soon have a new lover. Interestingly, some authorities have suggested that if the dreamer can identify the talisman he or she should adopt it as a lucky charm. The most recent dream research has concluded that the dream symbolises a difficult decision which is hanging over the dreamer, and should be resolved.

TAXES

Roman sources contain the first mention of dreams about taxes, and the reassuring omen that the dreamer will have enough to meet the demand. Later European authorities thought that a dream of paying taxes would bring an end to a current dispute; while to imagine being a tax collector augured for a beneficial change in life. The consensus of modern opinion now cites this as a dream of contrary: in Britain it predicts prosperous times ahead; while in America, to imagine filling in a tax return points to a salary increase!

TEA

Indian folklore associates tea with long life and prosperity; and with its increase in popularity throughout the world, dreams about tea have similarly come to symbolise happiness and conviviality. But some Victorian dream books did feel that to dream of brewing tea would lead the dreamer to be 'guilty of indiscreet actions'; while to spill tea pointed to some domestic upsets. Modern authorities have stated that to dream of people drinking tea foretells a round of social engagements, while the act of pouring a pot of tea indicates a steady flow of money in the future.

TEACHER
For several centuries, dreams of being a teacher were thought to symbolise sorrow, and to imagine being in charge of a class was a warning for the dreamer to control his or her temper! This was modified in the eighteenth century when it was claimed that for a man to dream of teaching foretold an invitation to a 'solemn occasion'; while a woman could expect a sudden change in her domestic situation. Modern authorities still believe there is a lesson to be learned from this dream: that the dreamer needs to resolve certain aims and objectives to experience success in life.

TEETH
Beautiful white teeth have always been seen as omens of happiness and prosperity, while decaying teeth are symptomatic of illness. The earliest sources indicate that a dream of having teeth pulled was actually a good sign for business deals; though to imagine them falling out indicated death. Victorian authorities modified this last omen to foretelling bad news, adding that a sight of black teeth pointed to a relative becoming sick. Since the development of hygienic dental care, a dream of having teeth filled is said to signify good news; being fitted with false teeth will result in unexpected help to get out of a difficult situation; and to dream of brushing teeth will resolve a recent problem that has been causing anxiety. Modern researchers believe a dream of losing teeth should first be interpreted as a literal warning to check whether attention is needed, and if not, then it may well symbolise a sense of 'toothlessness' in facing up to the demands and complexities of life.

TELEVISION
Just as television has become a feature of everyday life, so it

212

has increasingly been reported in dreams. Research has indicated that it is what is seen on the screen which is crucial to the omen, although the sensation of being made happy or sad by what is viewed is also important. Because TV has such an influence on modern attitudes, authorities are also agreed that as a dream symbol it is a warning to resist being overly influenced by other people.

THEATRE
Dreams of the theatre have a long tradition in Europe, where they are said to symbolise sociability. In Germany, to dream of attending the theatre alone will result in some new friends; while in Italy, to watch a performance in which women take most of the principal roles foretells a new love-affair. In Britain, a darkened theatre is said to presage a period of boredom; and a recent American almanac claims that attending a theatre with a group of people will result in a loss of money. Research suggests the dream is a warning about trying to hide the realities of life behind illusion.

THIRST
Greek sources refer to dreams of feeling very thirsty as omens of unhappiness, and the thirstier the dreamer the bigger the problems that lie ahead. In the seventeenth century, to dream of drinking until a thirst was quenched was said to foretell riches and contentment; while an almanac published in the following century stated that the dreamer who could not satisfy his thirst would be unable to fulfil his ambitions. Modern research has concluded that the sensation of being thirsty is symbolic of the dreamer's ability to face up to the problems of life, and only by slaking this thirst with great determination will ultimate success be achieved.

THRONE
A dream of a throne is another example of contrary, and

even the earliest sources were in agreement that the person who aspired to rule would be in for disappointment and perhaps even a fall in status. European sources claimed that to imagine sitting on a throne would lead to the loss of close friends. To dream of a king or pope on a throne pointed to a major problem ahead. Modern authorities believe this dream relates to social standing, and the higher a person imagines ascending without having earned the right, the harder he or she is likely to fall.

TIGER
The tiger has been a powerful dream image since biblical times, when it was first described as a symbolic of opposition. The earliest references say that a dream of a tiger advancing is an omen that the sleeper will be 'tormented and persecuted by enemies', unless he can beat off the animal before waking. In India, a tiger running presages an illness in the family; while a tiger eating means coming into some money. A recent American dream book claims that to see tigers performing in a circus is a sign of having helpful friends. Researchers have suggested that the dream is an encouragement to those faced by even the strongest adversary or obstacle that they can, with determination, succeed.

TOMB
The early civilisations believed dreams of tombs to be rather ill-omened, but later authorities have concluded that this is another dream of contrary: the older and more sinister-looking the tomb, the happier are the dreamer's prospects. Medieval documents claimed that the person who dreamed of wandering among tombs would soon get married, and to imagine being put into a tomb would bring an inheritance. A Victorian source reported that to read the inscriptions on a tomb foretold some unpleasant duties, but to dream of visiting a tomb with another person would herald the arrival of a new business partner.

214

TOYS

Toys have featured in the dreams of adults, as well as children, and are believed to be symbolic of pleasant new developments in life. European sources state that toys foretell family happiness, although to dream of giving them away will apparently result in being ostracised from society. Both British and American sources have reported that dreams of broken toys presage illness in the family. Modern research has further suggested that dreams of damaged toys are a warning to the sleeper against childish behaviour, as this could seriously affect their business and social life.

TRAFFIC

Very much a dream of the twentieth century with varying omens. European sources, for instance, claim that to dream of being in a traffic jam points to some happy days ahead; while in America it is symbolic of infidelity, and in Australia a loss of money. The heavier the traffic, said a recent French book of dream lore, the more active a social life the dreamer will lead, making new friends along the way. Modern research suggests this dream is symbolic of an increasing number of family problems, and the dreamer would do best to seek assistance rather than plod on alone.

TRAVEL

Dreams of travelling were first noted by the ancient Greeks, who declared that the omens were to be read from the land through which the dreamer passed — whether it was pleasant countryside or hostile terrain. Beautiful scenery foretold a happy domestic life, while barren land was a warning against dubious business deals. Dreams of travelling with other people — in particular family members — are good omens, according to European sources; while a recent British almanac claims that a dream of travel for pleasure will bring a welcome increase of income!

TREES

The omens relating to trees in dreams are truly universal; interestingly, many sources have referred to them taking on human, often female, shape. The old folk-legends describe trees springing from deep in the ground and towering up to the sky, and hence they came to symbolise man's highest aspirations and deepest roots when seen in dreams. Trees in full foliage are said to be omens of happiness and prosperity, while those which have fallen or been felled foretell sickness and trouble. To dream of planting a tree signifies a new love-affair; while the sight of a sapling is a very good omen for any change in life, such as a move of house or change of job. To dream of climbing up a tree indicates a new position in life; but to fall from one, a loss of money or a job. A recent survey has confirmed that the tree is one of the commonest of all dream symbols, representing at its most basic peace of mind.

TRIAL

For many years, dreams of trials were described as warnings of bad news. By the eighteenth century the news was said to relate specifically to the dreamer's family. In Europe another element was added — that the dream could also foretell an injustice being done to a relative or friend. A later American source has claimed that to dream of being unjustly accused at a trial is a sign of a very passionate love-life! Recent study has also suggested this dream is a caution against becoming involved in dubious ventures.

TUNNEL

Night visions of being in a darkened tunnel are now categorised as obstacle dreams, the omens being governed by whether the dreamer got out of the tunnel before awaking. The Romans, who were great tunnel builders, believed the dream was a bad omen for business and matters of the heart; while later generations said that a tunnel which caved in was a warning about enemies lying in wait.

216

European authorities believe that to dream of anything advancing in a tunnel — such as a train or a car — foretells ill health; while American sources claim this dream indicates that a secret is about to be revealed. The most recent research has concluded the dream is symbolic of difficulties, and the dreamer will need to take a risk in order to overcome.

TURKEY
Rural almanacs believe the turkey is symbolic of 'abundant gain', and whether the bird is alive, or prepared ready for the plate, the omens are for good luck and prosperity. In Europe, to dream of eating a turkey has for centuries been said to indicate a joyful occasion, though in America it is said to foretell infidelity! In Britain, to dream of a flock of turkeys strutting about gobbling is believed to herald an argument with friends.

U

UGLY

The ancient Egyptians first recorded dreams of ugliness, and decided that to see ugly people was an omen of a long and happy life. Not so lucky if the dreamer was the ugly one as this foretold problems with the opposite sex. The Greeks believed a dream of ugly people was a warning about the evil intentions of rivals or enemies, and this interpretation survived in many parts of the world until recent times. In Europe, to dream of ugly children is an omen of family arguments, while the young girl who imagines herself to be ugly is in danger of behaving badly towards her man, thus threatening their love-affair. Modern research suggests this dream symbolises a lack of self-confidence.

UMBRELLA

Chinese sources declared the umbrella to be a symbol of security, and believed that to dream of carrying one open over the head foretold pleasure and prosperity. Later European authorities were a little more sceptical, claiming that to carry a folded umbrella was a warning about a number of imminent little problems; while one that was broken or torn would result in the dreamer being maligned by friends. Most sources agree that an open umbrella in the house presages misfortune. Apart from the security aspect, an umbrella has also been seen as symbolising the opinions of other people, behind which the dreamer is hiding rather than asserting his or her own convictions.

UNDERGROUND
There are no indications whether the early cave-dwellers dreamed of living underground, and it is not until the seventeenth century that records mention this dream as symbolising distress and anxiety. A German almanac describes a dream of being underground as a warning against taking actions which will prove a threat to the dreamer's reputation. A very early twentieth-century American book of dream lore says this experience represents a subconscious desire to undermine the achievements of others. Modern sources say a dream of travelling underground, such as on the underground railway or metro, is a warning against a risky speculation.

UNDERTAKER
The men who deal with the dead have been cited in dream lore as cases of contrary since the days of the Greek and Roman Empires. To have need of an undertaker was said to be a sign of happiness, while to dream of visiting his premises was a promise of long life. Later European authorities have added that the undertaker is symbolic of a birth or a wedding, although one recent American almanac claims that to dream of being an undertaker will result in the death of a relative.

UNDERWEAR
Dreams of pretty and enticing underwear are common to both sexes, and modern sources have provided a number of omens. Silk or nylon underwear is symbolic of financial luck; cotton represents pleasure; and wool signifies security. To dream of putting on new underwear presages an exciting adventure, while taking it off will result in several important changes in the dreamer's life. To imagine doing a

striptease (according to an American source) indicates the dreamer has a great desire to do good for others.

UNDRESSING
In the Middle Ages, a dream of undressing was said to foretell a visit from a loved one, though to imagine undressing in public pointed to misery and distress. The Victorians naturally took a high moral tone where this subject was concerned: a woman who dreamed of undressing would become the object of 'scandalous gossip'; while the man who imagined a woman undressing would be 'guilty of stolen pleasures which will rebound with grief'. Modern authorities have placed less sexual implication on this dream, believing that to dream of the opposite sex undressing is a warning about confiding in new friends. For either a man or woman to undress signifies a love that is not going to be returned by the object of that affection. In America, any dream of undressing in a public place or in front of other people, apart from partners or lovers, is the sign a secret is about to be revealed. A recent almanac has also claimed that to dream of undressing in a hotel room indicates satisfaction in love.

UNFAITHFUL
Nineteenth-century French books of dream lore were in no doubt that to dream of a lover or partner being unfaithful was the reverse of the truth: for very soon after, the dream evidence of their faithfulness would manifest itself. Later European almanacs have reported that if either men or women dream of being unfaithful *themselves*, then they will be tempted to do so but could well end up a double loser. Several modern authorities have suggested the dream could also be a warning that someone, not necessarily of the opposite sex, is taking advantage of the dreamer's trust.

UNHAPPY
A dream of unhappiness is another of the classic contrary

sleep experiences. Authorities are agreed that the more miserable the dreamer imagines himself to be, the better his prospects for fun and enjoyment. It is also said that married couples dreaming of being unhappy together will actually enjoy a great deal of pleasure; while seeing children unhappy presages some good news which will be received in a letter. Lovers being unhappy with each other are also apparently going to receive an invitation by mail to a big social occasion, says a recent American source.

UNIFORM

Since the days of the Roman Empire, a uniform has been regarded as symbolic of social prominence and good fortune. In the Middle Ages, dreams of seeing people in strange uniforms were believed to be omens of war, or possibly family disruptions. By the eighteenth century, to dream of men in uniforms presaged a rise in social status, though women who imagined themselves in uniforms were warned against conferring their favours unwisely. Interestingly, a recent American almanac suggests that today's girl who dreams of wearing a uniform at work is being warned against becoming arrogant. The consensus of modern opinions on this dream is that it is a warning against blindly conforming to the ideas of others, regardless of personal convictions.

UNIVERSITY

European sources, as early as the Middle Ages, described any dreams of a university to be a good omen, especially if the dreamer was a student or engaged in any kind of research, for it augured well for success. In America, too, the dream is considered to be a pleasing confirmation of the dreamer's talents, regardless of whether he or she is actually attending a university. British sources, likewise accept this definition, though they do believe that ultimate success will have to be backed up by determination and effort.

URINE

The earliest records indicate that urine was equated with seminal fluid, and considered a symbol of creative power and strength. The Assyrian *Book of Dreams* stated that if a man imagined his urine forming a stream that struck a wall and then spread into the street, he would have children; if he aimed at the sky his son would become an important person; but if the water fell into a well he would lose his property. Should the luckless sleeper urinate on himself then he would become ill. Later European authorities said that any dream of urinating promised business success; while to see children passing water foretold prosperity. A quaint Victorian dream book claimed that for either a man or woman to dream of urinating signified domestic harmony; and to see a urinal pot beside the bed indicated a flow of material gains! Although Freud stated that urinary symbolism was the same as sexual symbolism, most researchers now agree that this quite commonplace dream is symbolic of virility and vitality.

V

VACCINATION

An increasingly common dream in recent years, which authorities are inclined to believe symbolises insincerity. Dream books of the 1920s claimed that the man who imagined being vaccinated was about to fall victim to the wiles of an unscrupulous female; while for either sex, it has been suggested in America that the dreamer is showering affections on an unworthy person. Children being vaccinated are a warning against wasting money on dubious ventures.

VAGINA

For a woman to dream of having a diseased vagina was seen, in the Middle Ages, as a warning against casual sexual relations, and modern authorities have found no reason to change this verdict. Early writers also believed that for a woman to imagine exposing her genitalia was a similar caution against indiscretions. A related dream of having no vagina was initially thought to be symbolic of being infertile, but more recent research has concluded that this indicates a problem in the dreamer's sex life, and she should seek professional advice.

VALLEY

Another of the classic dreams. For centuries a green and pleasant valley has been said to symbolise contentment and ease, while a barren and isolated one points to a future of sickness and problems. Medieval documents claimed that a valley full of wildlife symbolised prosperity and friendship; while children at play in a valley indicated the sleeper would receive some money sooner than expected. Modern research has further suggested that the dream of a beautiful valley should be seen as an encouragement for the dreamer to fulfil his or her potential. A bleak valley symbolises anxiety, which can be resolved by firm decision-making.

VALUABLES

Dreams of losing valuables, such as a handbag, a wallet, some money or any other similar item, are another very commonplace experience. The first thing the dreamer should do on waking is to check and make sure that the item is indeed not missing, for this could well be a case of subliminal perception. If the valuable object does prove to be missing, recall where the loss took place in the dream, and begin any search there. The early authorities believed this dream to be a warning about a future loss or theft, although by the eighteenth century it was regarded more as a warning about losing *values* in life rather than money. Dreams of finding money and valuables are also widely reported, and any omens from such a dream — like a possible location — should be immediately investigated. If the recovered property belongs to someone else then do the decent thing and return it! If nothing comes to light, then the dream is believed to symbolise a feeling of not being fully 'valued' by family or friends.

VAMPIRE

The suave vampire of modern films and books is far removed from the emaciated, living-dead person of legend; and among the curious omens which have been attributed to this creature, in dreams, is that they symbolise a desire to marry for money! Victorian almanacs claimed that dreams of vampires should not be regarded as nightmares but actually as examples of contrary: they would be followed by good news, probably of a financial nature. Modern research suggests that any dream of a vampire-like creature intent on sucking blood, is a symbol of an emotional crisis which requires professional guidance.

VEGETABLES

The omens concerning vegetables in dreams vary considerably, although fresh ones denote good health. Some early European authorities believed they indicated hard work with very little return for all the labour involved; while to eat them presaged an unsettled period of life. In Britain, cooking vegetables in a dream indicates a long wait for success, and bad vegetables point to a period of disappointment. In America, vegetables are believed to be symbolic of economy and the enjoyment of simple, everyday things. To dream of growing vegetables signifies domestic harmony.

VEIL

In the East, the veil has been regarded as a symbol of mystery and modesty for centuries, though with the passage of time it has come to have a stronger sexual connotation in the West. For example, dreams of veiled women were for a time believed to signify the dreamer was just being a little secretive about personal matters; but by the eighteenth century the veil had become synonymous with sexual adventures. The woman who dreamed of putting on a veil was planning to deceive her husband or lover; while if she took it off she was inviting seduction. A torn veil was a warning that an illicit affair was about to be discovered; while to lose one signified that a minor embarrassment was all that the dreamer would suffer despite committing a major indiscretion! Modern authorities agree that the dream is symbolic of a tussle between the dreamer and his or her sexual libido.

VILLAGE

To imagine being back in the village of your birth is a very happy dream, which rural almanacs during the past three centuries have said foretells good health and a number of pleasant surprises; in particular, being reunited with some old friends. In biblical times, to dream of a village was said to be a portent of a change for the better in the dreamer's circumstances. In medieval England, to imagine a neglected village was symbolic of poverty. Curiously, a burning village was believed to foretell going on a pilgrimage. Modern authorities are agreed that a dream of the country village symbolises achievement, and a coastal village indicates unexpected gain.

VINES

The Romans believed dreams of vines to be very good omens, especially if they were weighed down with grapes — said to signify having many good friends. Full-bodied and succulent fruit was also said to indicate a vigorous sex life. A withered vine pointed to hard times ahead, while one that had been stripped of all its fruit signified the dreamer was in danger of becoming the victim of a plausible but illegal scheme. Modern authorities have also suggested that a withered vine could be symbolic of the dreamer having overtaxed his or her strength.

VIRGINS

The ancient Greeks believed that a dream of a virgin augured well for 'speculations', and several other early authorities refer to dreams of embracing a virgin as symbolising 'great happiness'. Medieval records mention dreams of kidnapping virgins, which would result in imprisonment; and a seventeenth-century document pointed out that the man who dreamed of taking a young girl's virginity 'would fail in all his enterprises and be cast out from among his fellow men'. Victorian books of dream lore cautioned their female readers that the girl who dreamed of losing her viginity was endangering her reputation; while the married woman who dreamed of regaining her virginity would be unhappy in her family and social life.

VISIT
One of the most straightforward of dreams, for if the visit was a pleasure then expect the same in real life; if it was unpleasant in any way, then beware of problems created by a malicious person. To be visited by friends foretells some good news; though for the dreamer to be a member of a party of visitors is a warning against being exploited by flattery. A visitor who is pale and drawn presages illness, according to a British source, especially if the visitor is a woman. In America, to dream of being visited by some businessmen is said to indicate a lawsuit is on the way!

VOLCANO
The earliest oracles wrote that the omen for a dream of a smoking volcano was that it signified a passionate love-affair — but one based on deceit! Over the years, volcanos have become widely associated with sex: an eighteenth-century almanac, for instance, declared that the young girl who dreamed of an active volcano would be driven by selfishness and greed to 'entrap a husband by shamelessly using her charms'. A man having this same dream would also pursue women with equal disregard for the finer feel-ings, says a Victorian source. An exploding volcano is now viewed by a number of dream researchers as a symbol of lust; and without a certain degree of restraint this could become a dangerous obsession.

VOYAGE
Dreams of voyaging go back to the days of antiquity, and the consensus of opinion is that they foretell receiving an inheritance rather than actually going travelling. Curiously, most dreams of voyages seem to be taken alone

— which is in no way ill-omened — for according to one European source, being accompanied by another person, particularly a female, indicates becoming the subject of a rather nasty campaign of gossip.

W

WAGES
Payment of money in return for labour has been a constant theme in dreams since the days of the Roman Empire, and once again the omens are a case of contrary: to receive money presages a loss or theft; while to give it to others points to a beneficial change in life. In Europe, there are records of dreams in which wages were reduced, and these were believed to be a warning about the machinations of enemies; while an increase was regarded as a bad omen for any new undertaking. In Britain, this century, dreams relating to salary have continued to be seen as cases of opposite: to be refused a salary increase will produce money from an unexpected source; though to be granted a rise is believed to be a warning about missing out on promotion, unless more effort is made.

WAITERS
The old omens that were applied to dreams of servants have been reapplied to waiters and waitresses. In general terms, to see anyone involved in serving food is an indication to the dreamer that he or she will shortly be entertained by a friend. But, if the service is less than satisfactory then the omen is of an illness of a relative. Some authorities believe the dream also indicates that the sleeper could be

doing too much for others who are well able to help themselves — *or vice versa*!

WALKING

Dreams of walking are very much goverened by circumstances, and most authorities agree that they are another
example of obstacle — where the conclusion governs the
omens. The earliest records describe the dream as being
symbolic of achievement, with good luck and prosperity
being the outcome of a stroll through pleasant countryside.
A walk at night, or over rough terrain — particularly where
there are brambles and other obstacles — points to health
problems and a struggle to find peace of mind. In the
eighteenth century, a dream of walking fast was believed to
be an appeal to resolve pressing matters; while the sensation of walking very slowly, or even backwards, would
lead to a loss of money. Modern authorities are agreed that
the dream is a clear suggestion that determination and
patience are necessary for the dreamer to realise his or her
ambitions.

WALLS

Walls have long been regarded as classic examples of obstacle dreams, and it is necessary to surmount them in
order to avoid trouble. The Romans suggested that to jump
over a wall would enable the dreamer to achieve his or her
ambitions, and also believed that a dream of a wall indicated financial security. Medieval sources claimed that to
dream of demolishing a wall would lead to the overthrow of
enemies; but to dream of falling off one would result in a lot
of hard and unnecessary work. For either a man or woman
to dream of hiding behind a wall signifies they are nursing a
guilty secret, according to modern sources.

WAR

Another dream that has troubled mankind since the days of
antiquity, though the omens of misfortune and a danger of

illness are believed to apply to the dreamer *personally* rather than nations as a whole. Greek oracles claimed that a dream of war foretold domestic problems for couples, while the young maiden who dreamed of her lover going to war would hear something detrimental about his character. In the Middle Ages, to dream of a country at war was a warning against dubious trading deals, although to win a war would produce some excellent financial news. Most modern sources believe any dream of war is symbolic of a persecution complex.

WASHING

Washing the hands is another very old dream sensation and has always been seen as indicating the start of a new friendship. The earliest sources claimed it was important that the water was clear, with cold water being symbolic of contentment and hot water of success. The people of the Middle Ages believed a dream of washing the body was a sign of immoral conduct; while to wash the feet indicated anxiety. More recent enquiry has concluded that the dreamer who imagines washing clothes is being warned about getting entangled in the affairs of other people. However, to dream of washing dishes is a happy omen of being visited by friends!

WATER

Water, the original womb and source of life, is symbolic of abundance in dreams, and as an omen it has been looked upon as fortuitous since records of this kind were first kept. Clear water is a sign of prosperity, while dirty water fortells illness. The early oracles claimed that a dream of drawing water indicated happiness, but to spill water would lead to a quarrel. Flood water is a warning against being swept into evil ways, though splashing or playing in water signifies 'an awakening of love and passion', according to a Victorian almanac. Curiously, a dream of a waterfall foretells achieving a long-held ambition, but to imagine picking watercress is a warning against promiscuous sex! A consensus of modern opinion sees water as a link with the maternal subconscious, representing an opportunity for change in life.

WEALTH
One of the most famous dreams of contrary: the wealthier the dreamer imagines himself to be, the greater the danger of financial problems, plus the likelihood of complications in matters of the heart. Since biblical times, to dream of other people being wealthy is an assurance that the dreamer has good friends, who may well come to his or her aid in times of need. A medieval document claimed that the rich person who dreamed of marrying a poor one was about to fall ill; while several nineteenth-century almanacs forecast that the poor person who dreamed of marrying into wealth could expect to earn good wages. Modern research suggests that this may well be a dream of aspirations beyond a person's abilities.

WEAVING
In the Middle Ages, a dream of weaving was held to be very auspicious and signified a happy and prosperous life. To be the weaver was a forecast of peace of mind; though any hitches that might be encountered while working on the loom should be regarded as small domestic problems, and these would be overcome with the goodwill of all the family members. A quaint eighteenth-century almanac described a dream of seeing people weaving as a sign that the sleeper would be 'surrounded by healthy and energetic conditions'. A recent American authority has suggested the dream is synonymous with earning money.

WEDDING
Although dream records indicate this to be a widely reported experience, it certainly does *not* portend a wedding for the dreamer, her family or friends. Indeed, for

many centuries it has been said to be symbolic of a period of happiness — and if the 'dream' marriage was that of a relative, then the happiness could well be provided by a financial windfall. The Victorians believed that any unmarried person who dreamed of a wedding was damaging her own chances of marital bliss; but if a young girl imagined her lover marrying someone else it actually augured well for their own relationship.

WHALE
It is a good sign that international concern is now being expressed about the hunting and killing of this huge mammal — because for several centuries they have been regarded in dreams as an omen of protection. The creature was not so favourably regarded in earlier times — perhaps because of the association with Jonah — and to dream of one approaching a ship was said to threaten a loss of property; while nautical almanacs claimed that if a whale attacked a ship it would throw the dreamer into 'a whirlpool of disasters'. Today, a dream of a whale is said to indicate a pleasing achievement in social or business life despite considerable opposition. Some authorities have also claimed that the whale has a feminine significance because of its enormous cavities, and to dream of being swallowed up and regurgitated can augur a whole new life.

WHEELS
The wheel has been a strong dream symbol since the days of the Roman Empire: one spinning quickly indicated success in business; and even a slow-moving wheel predicted achievement, as long as enough effort was being put in. A broken wheel, however, presaged a death or the unexpected absence of someone from the dreamer's home. The omens regarding wheels on the various different forms of transport should be consulted in the appropriate sections of this book. It should be added that a recent American

survey has concluded that to see a gambling wheel in action will bring about a most embarrassing situation!

WHISKY
Whisky has always been symbolic of prosperity to the Scots, though a number of earlier dream books believed it to be rather ill-omened. A seventeenth-century European work, for instance, describes a dream of drinking whisky as foretelling 'bad events to come', while an American almanac of the following century claimed that to buy whisky would result in debts and difficulties. The Victorians took a predictably moralistic tone, stating that a dream of offering whisky to a lover would result in temptation. Today's authorities believe whisky to be a symbol of success — when being drunk in moderation.

WILL
To dream of making a will is not regarded by experts as an omen of death, but rather another case of contrary where the dreamer can disregard any worries he may be having about his health. A nineteenth-century European source claimed that to dream of writing out a will signified a number of interesting speculations; while to lose a will was a bad omen for business affairs. A Victorian almanac stated that to destroy a will would lay the dreamer open to treachery and deceit. Any dream of another person's will points to family problems, says a recent British report.

WIND
The Arabs held the wind in great respect, for they believed that horses, so invaluable to their existence, had been created from the condensation of the south wind; they therefore believed that any sensation of wind in a dream symbolised energy and transformation. The Chinese, too, said that to dream of the wind signified a time of change and an opportune moment to begin new ventures. According to European almanacs, a gentle breeze predicts good

news, while a strong wind points to hard work ahead. A gusty wind, however, signifies a period of frustration in home or business life.

WINDOW
Previous generations took a lot of interest in dreams about windows, seeing them as either opening onto better things, or closed by disappointment and failure. Early sources described a dream of a wide open window as a pointer to success, while a shut or broken window indicated being deserted by family or friends. An eighteenth-century European authority stated that a dream of sitting in a window was a warning against foolish actions; while to see other people at a window would result in a family disagreement, probably over money. Modern sources believe a dream of staring through a window is symbolic of looking for guidance, but actually to jump out of one points to finding a solution to the problem!

WINE
The Greeks and Romans believed that wine was symbolic of prosperity and friendship, and to see barrels of wine in a cellar foretold some happy social gatherings. Spilling wine, though, was a bad omen signifying the spilling of blood. In the Middle Ages, to dream of making wine was an omen of good business — especially if it was white wine — though to dream of pouring it from one vessel to another indicated a journey. Modern sources have continued to accept the good omens about wine, adding, however, that to imagine breaking a bottle is a caution against leading an excessively lusty sex life!

WOODS
Medieval British records state that dreams of being lost in a wood were considered ill-omened as they symbolised that the dreamer would encounter a lot of unexpected obstacles in life. The same source adds that 'rich people dreaming of

being in woods will lose money', though poor people would prosper. Later European authorities, however, claimed that to see a wood thick with trees pointed to a number of pleasant social engagements; while a fire in a wood curiously signfied the maturity of current plans. In America, this omen is quite the reverse if the trees appear to have been recently burned. Most modern authorities accept that to see other people in a wood is a warning to be cautious in business affairs.

WOMEN
Controversially, the earliest authorities stated that to dream of a woman was a symbol of jealousy and intrigue, and to imagine a group of females together, signified treachery and deceit! Long before the Middle Ages, however, these omens had been superseded; and women in dreams were said to indicate security in love. To see one naked foretold great happiness. Sometime around the sixteenth century, blonde women were described as symbolising long life, while brunettes indicated honour and prosperity. Later almanacs added that a pregnant woman represented financial gain and a dancing woman illness, although a woman with hair down to her ankles signified adultery. Modern authorities believe it is the surroundings in which the woman or women are seen that is crucial to the omen — and if she speaks, the message may be more important still.

WORK
Man has always believed that dreams of hard work symbolised success and achievement in business, and to see others at work similarly augured well for home and family life. In the eighteenth-century, the workhouse, far from being looked upon as the grim and forbidding place it was, earned the reputation, in dreams, of being an example of contrary: the dreamer could expect good luck as well as coming into some money! The modern workshop is

similarly believed to be a sign to the dreamer that he should exploit his talents and ingenuity to the fullest.

WRINKLES
Several eighteenth-century books of dream lore confirm what was believed to be a much older omen, that dreams of having wrinkles were a sign of a long and prosperous life. Young people who dreamed of having wrinkles were cautioned against vanity, though in the case of men this foretold business losses through lack of attention to detail. Modern authorities believe any dream of wrinkles actually indicates an improved social life; the dreamer is being gently reminded that beauty is only skin deep — the mind is what really matters and attracts friendship.

WRITING
Some old sources have stated that a dream of writing was a warning about a forthcoming mistake that could seriously affect the dreamer's future. If the writing was illegible it was a sign to be on guard against enemies. A nineteenth-century European almanac advised readers that to dream of writing a love-letter indicated happiness, writing a business letter would produce profits, while a letter to friends should result in several social engagements. Recent study has concluded it may be possible to remember enough of what was written to determine the significance of the dream. If not, says a British authority, it could be a simple reminder that the dreamer owes someone a letter!

X Y Z

XENOPHOBIA

Dreams of xenophobia — hatred of foreigners — are first recorded in the early eighteenth century, where they are listed as examples of contrary: the stronger the hatred felt, the greater the happiness that the dreamer will enjoy. The Victorian books of dream lore listed several specific races as being the main objects of xenophobia (these included the French, Germans and Jews), but stated that no matter which nationality the dreamer imagined, the omens were the same — a family quarrel. A French almanac claimed, earlier this century, that to dream of insulting a foreigner signified that a mystery was about to be solved; while a recent American publication has stated that to see a foreigner being deported will result in the loss of a close friend.

YACHT

Nautical almanacs report that the yacht is symbolic of endeavour, and to dream of one of these graceful craft at sea, under full sail, augurs well for the dreamer's future in business and family life. A Victorian dream book claimed that this same dream indicated getting the opportunity to have some recreation away from business problems, but added that if the yacht was beached, or stranded, then the problems would get worse. To sail a yacht on a choppy sea points to the fulfilment of ambitions, with the possibility of a financial bonus. Modern sources have added that the dream can equally well be interpreted as an urge to travel.

YAWNING
The Chinese believed dreams in which people yawned were very ill-omened, presaging ill health and death. Ancient legends, which spoke of the soul leaving the body during a yawn, are believed to have inspired this definition which spread from the East to the West. Later European oracles declared that the dream symbolised a vain search for health and contentment. By the nineteenth century, it was widely believed that to imagine other people yawning was a sign that a member of the family was going to fall dangerously ill. An American dream almanac published in the early 1900s stated that to dream of yawning at a social function would lead a young man to be jilted by his girlfriend. In Australia, this same experience will result in a public humiliation. Recent research suggests this dream is symbolic of laziness and negative thinking.

YOUTH
To dream of being young again was first reported by the ancient Babylonians who interpreted it as a sign of forthcoming important news. The Romans believed the dream was a hint to take advantage of opportunities before it became too late — a definition that many modern authorities still accept. Other early sources have stated that to dream of young people is a prognostication that the time is right for resolving family disagreements; while for either a husband or wife to imagine their partner young again is a confirmation of the steadfastness of their love.

ZIGZAG
The sensation of zigzagging while walking or, equally, wandering through a maze, has been noted by several books of dream lore during the past 200 years, where

it is said to be a warning about forthcoming emotional problems in the dreamer's family. One nineteenth-century almanac even went as far as to say it signified madness! Modern research has, however, declared the dream to be symbolic of hesitancy and a loss of direction in life. Thus, the dreamer should be encouraged to be decisive in his or her decisions as this will result in a real turning-point in life.

ZIPPER

The thought of having an undone zipper on a pair of trousers or a skirt is a familiar enough feeling in life, but in dreams it is a warning about becoming unduly casual in relationships. Certainly, any dream of this kind is a warning of embarrassment — probably in the form of some unwelcome news concerning an illicit relationship. It is a topic that has perhaps naturally provoked some light-hearted comments in books of dream lore. A recent American publication, for instance, suggesting that to unzip clothes indicates good health; while the man who dreams of unzipping a woman's garments (or vice versa) will soon receive 'riches'!

ZODIAC

Interest in star signs can be traced back to the ancient Greeks who evolved the idea of the zodiac, and it was they who first defined dreams about it as symbolising good fortune. Although any dream of the zodiac was said to foretell a rise in status, the chance of riches went to the dreamer who witnessed his or her *own* sign. A number of European writers have said that to dream of drawing a zodiac sign signifies some unspecified good luck, but if the sign swirls about and becomes disjointed, then there is the danger of an illness. In any event, consulting star signs in the waking hours is likely to be far more revealing than during sleep!